100% NEW

DEVELOPING MATHEMATICS

**Customisable
teaching resources
for mathematics**

USING AND APPLYING MATHEMATICS

Ages 7–8

Hil... and ...lls

A & C Black • London

Contents

UNIVERSITY OF CHICHESTER

Solve one-step and two-step problems involving numbers, money or measures, including time, choosing and carrying out appropriate calculations

Represent the information in a puzzle or problem using numbers, images or diagrams; use these to find a solution and present it in context, where appropriate using £.p notation or units of measure

Follow a line of enquiry by deciding what information is important; make and use lists, tables and graphs to organise and interpret the information

Identify patterns and relationships involving numbers or shapes, and use these to solve problems

Describe and explain methods, choices and solutions to puzzles and problems, orally and in writing, using pictures and diagrams

Published 2009 by A&C Black Publishers Limited
36 Soho Square, London W1D 3QY
www.acblack.com

ISBN 978-1-4081-1311-0

Copyright text © Hilary Koll and Steve Mills 2009
Copyright illustrations © Sean Longcroft 2009
Copyright cover illustration © Piers Baker 2009
Editor: Marie Lister
Designed by Billin Design Solutions Ltd

The author and publishers would like to thank Catherine Yemm and Judith Wells for their advice in producing this series of books.

A CIP catalogue record for this book is available from the British Library.

Printed and bound in Great Britain by Halstan Printing Group.

A&C Black uses paper produced with elemental chlorine-free pulp, harvested from managed sustainable forests.

Introduction

100% New Developing Mathematics: Using and Applying Mathematics is a series of seven photocopiable activity books for children aged 4 to 11, designed to be used during the daily maths lesson. The books focus on the skills and concepts for Using and Applying Mathematics as outlined in the Primary National Strategy *Primary Framework for literacy and mathematics*. The activities are intended to be used in the time allocated to pupil activities in the daily maths lesson. They aim to reinforce the knowledge and develop the skills and understanding explored during the main part of the lesson, and to provide practice and consolidation of the learning objectives contained in the Framework document.

Using and Applying Mathematics

There are several different components which make up the **content** of maths and form the bulk of any maths curriculum:

- **mathematical facts**, for example a triangle has three sides;
- **mathematical skills**, such as counting;
- **mathematical concepts**, like place value.

For maths teaching to be successful, it is vital that children can use this mathematical content beyond their classroom, either in real-life situations or as a basis for further understanding. However, in order to do so they require extra abilities over and above the mathematical content they have learned. These extra abilities are often referred to as the **processes** of mathematical activity. It is these processes which make mathematical content usable.

As an example, consider this question:

How many triangles are there in this shape?

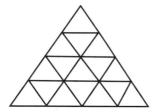

The mathematical 'content' required is only:

- the **fact** that a triangle has three sides;
- the **skill** of counting.

As such, it could be expected that very young children could solve this problem. The fact that they cannot, suggests that other abilities are involved. These are the processes, and for this question they include:

- visualising the different-sized triangles;
- being systematic in counting all the triangles of different sizes;
- looking for patterns in the numbers of triangles;
- trial and error;
- recording.

Unless children can apply these processes in this situation, then however good their counting skills and knowledge of triangles may be, they will fail.

The strand 'Using and Applying Mathematics' of the *Primary Framework for mathematics* emphasises the importance of using and talking about the mathematics in real situations. This series of books is intended to make more explicit the processes involved in learning how to put one's maths to use.

Using and Applying Mathematics Ages 7–8 supports the development of the using and applying processes by providing a series of activities that provide opportunities to introduce and practise them through a series of activities. On the whole the activities are designed for children to work on independently, either individually, in pairs or in groups.

Pre-school children are naturally inquisitive about the world around them. They like to explore and experiment, and to make marks and record things on paper in their own idiosyncratic ways. At school, the focus is sometimes on the maths 'content' alone and children can believe that maths is not a subject of exploration, but rather one of simply learning the 'right way to do things'. As a result, when older children are asked to explore and investigate maths they are often at a loss.

Ages 7–8 helps children to develop the following processes:

- predicting
- explaining
- visualising
- being systematic
- looking for pattern
- co-operating
- recording
- comparing
- reasoning
- testing ideas
- making decisions
- trial and improvement
- estimating
- asking own questions

When using these activities, the focus need not be on the actual mathematical 'content'. Instead, the teacher's demonstrations, discussions and questioning should emphasise the processes the children are using. When appropriate, invite the children to explain their thinking to others. Research has shown that children develop processes most successfully when the teacher encourages pupils to act as experts rather than novices, granting them more autonomy, and encouraging a range of approaches to any problem. The children should evaluate their own plans against other plans in the posing, planning and monitoring phases of the lessons.

Ages 7–8 helps children with Solving Problems, Representing, Enquiring, Reasoning and Communicating, as recommended in the revised Primary Framework. These five themes, although identified separately in the table below, are interlinked.

Using and applying mathematics	Solving problems	Representing	Enquiring	Reasoning	Communicating
Year 3	Solve one-step and two-step problems involving numbers, money or measures, including time, choosing and carrying out appropriate calculations	Represent the information in a puzzle or problem using numbers, images or diagrams; use these to find a solution and present it in context, where appropriate using £.p notation or units of measure	Follow a line of enquiry by deciding what information is important; make and use lists, tables and graphs to organise and interpret the information	Use patterns and relationships involving numbers or shapes, and use these to solve problems	Describe and explain methods, choices and solutions to puzzles and problems, orally and in writing, using pictures and diagrams

Extension

Many of the activity sheets end with a challenge (**Now try this!**), which reinforces and extends children's learning, and provides the teacher with an opportunity for assessment. These might include harder questions, with numbers from a higher range than those in the main part of the activity sheet. Some challenges are open-ended questions and provide opportunity for children to think mathematically for themselves. Occasionally the challenge will require additional paper or that the children write on the reverse of the sheet itself. Many of the activities encourage children to generate their own questions or puzzles for a partner to solve.

Organisation

Very little equipment is needed, but it will be useful to have available: coloured pencils, 100-squares, 0–9 numeral cards, geared clocks, dice, scissors, glue/sticky tape, coins (£2, £1, 50p, 20p, 10p, 5p, 2p, 1p), centimetre squared paper, number lines, dice.

Where possible, the children's work should be supported by ICT equipment, such as number lines and tracks on interactive whiteboards, or computer software for comparing and ordering numbers. It is also vital that children's experiences are introduced in real-life contexts and through practical activities. The teachers' notes at the foot of each page and the more detailed notes on pages 6 to 11 suggest ways in which this can be done effectively.

To help teachers select appropriate learning experiences for the children, the activities are grouped into sections within the book. However, the activities are not expected to be used in this order unless stated otherwise. The sheets are intended to support, rather than direct, the teacher's planning.

Some activities can be made easier or more challenging by masking or substituting numbers. You may wish to re-use pages by copying them onto card and laminating them.

Accompanying CD

The enclosed CD-ROM contains all of the activity sheets from the book and a program that allows you to edit them for printing or saving. This means that modifications can be made to further differentiate the activities to suit individual pupils' needs. See page 12 for further details.

Teachers' notes

Brief notes are provided at the foot of each page, giving ideas and suggestions for maximising the effectiveness of the activity sheets. These can be masked before copying.

Further explanations of the activities can be found on pages 6 to 11, together with examples of questions that you can ask.

Whole class warm-up activities

The following activities provide some practical ideas that can be used to introduce or reinforce the main teaching part of the lesson, or provide an interesting basis for discussion.

What's my number?

Write a number on a sticky note and stick it to a child's forehead so they are unable to read it. Ask other children to give clues about the identity of the number, for example 'It's less than 10,' 'It's more than 6,' 'It is a multiple of 3,' 'It is even'.

What's it worth?

Give each child a set of 0–9 digit cards. Ask questions like: 'Hold up a number where the tens digit is worth 50.' 'Show me a number with 8 in the units place.' 'Hold up a number where the hundreds digit is worth 700.' 'Hold up a number between 450 and 500.' 'Hold up a number that is closer to 750 than to 700.'

Guess my shape

Pick a shape from a bag of flat shapes but do not show it to the children. They can ask three questions, for example 'Does it have five corners?', to which you answer 'Yes' or 'No'. A more difficult version involves playing the game using 3-D shapes.

Odd, odd, odd

This activity encourages the children to work systematically. Write the number 15 on the board. Ask them to suggest ways of adding three odd numbers to make 15, for example 1 + 5 + 9, 11 + 3 + 1. Write correct suggestions in a list and prompt the children to look for more. 'How many threes have we written? How many nines? Are we missing any?' Begin to organise the list so all the number sentences beginning with 1 come together, for example 1 + 3 + 11, 1 + 5 + 9. Discuss whether a digit can be used more than once, such as 3 + 3 + 9.

Notes on the activities

Understanding shape

Solve one-step and two-step problems involving numbers, money or measures, including time, choosing and carrying out appropriate calculations

This aspect of Using and Applying Mathematics deals with Solving Problems. It is central to all mathematics and if children are unable to solve problems then the mathematics that they know is wasted. Children need to develop confidence in tackling problems without looking to teachers or other children for help. They should learn to decide which facts are key to the problem, make decisions about what operations to use and then follow them through, checking to see if their answer is a sensible one.

Chocolate matters (page 13)

Processes: make decisions, record, reason, explain

These problems require the children to make their own decisions as to how to answer the questions. They should be encouraged to describe these methods and strategies and demonstrate how different equipment such as 100-squares, and number lines, could be used to help them reach answers.

SUGGESTED QUESTIONS:

- How did you work out the answer to this question?
- How did you know what to do?
- Can you show me how you could use a number line to reach the answer?

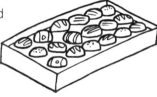

Fruit corner (page 14)

Processes: reason, record, make decisions

Allow the children to make their own decisions about what to do and encourage them to use number sentences or pictorial methods to record their working.

SUGGESTED QUESTIONS:

- How did you find this solution?
- How could you write this as a number sentence?

Two numbers (page 15)

Processes: look for pattern, reason, explain

Observe the methods children use to find the answers, for example noting which children use pictures, their fingers, equipment or a mental method. Revise the terms 'product' and 'total' and ask the children to work together to discuss their strategies.

SUGGESTED QUESTIONS:

- How did you find this solution?
- What does the word product mean?
- How could you write these as two number sentences?

Spiders and flies (page 16)

Processes: explain, ask own questions, reason

This activity can help the children to see how many different questions can be asked about a context and encourages them to make up their own questions.

SUGGESTED QUESTIONS:

- How many different questions have we asked in our class?
- How would you answer Jo's question?

The Street (page 17)

Processes: reason, make decisions, explain

Discuss strategies that the children chose to work out the answers, drawing attention to use of equipment such as number lines, 100-squares, materials or other methods or known number facts.

SUGGESTED QUESTIONS:

- How did you find the answer?
- What method did you use to find the answer?
- Did you use the same method for each question or did you do anything different on this question?

Pick 3 cards (page 18)

Processes: record, make decisions, explain

Begin the lesson by reminding children of the pounds and pence notation and asking them to find the total of 35p and £1.28. Discuss different strategies and remind them that they should either work with both numbers in pounds or with both in pence. The prices on the sheet could be changed before copying.

SUGGESTED QUESTIONS:

- How easy did you find this?
- Did you find the answer straight away?
- How did you work it out?

At the ice rink (page 19)

Processes: reason, make decisions, record

Children should work in pairs and record calculations for each problem to show what they think should be done. Remind them to use the correct unit in their answers where appropriate. Discuss differences in the calculations they write.

- How did you find this solution?
- Have you written the same number sentences as Jo?

Express pizza (page 20)

Processes: reason, explain, record

Children could work together in pairs on this activity to promote discussion. Talk about strategies for answering each question, for example adding £5 and subtracting 1p when adding £4.99.

SUGGESTED QUESTIONS:
- How did you find this solution?
- What strategies did you use?

Loop the loop (page 21)

Processes: reason, make decisions

At the start of the lesson, remind the children about the notation kg and g and that 1000 g is the same as 1 kg.

SUGGESTED QUESTIONS:
- How did you find this solution?
- If you can't find the answer, is it because the answer is in grams rather than kilograms?

Record breakers (page 22)

Processes: reason, make decisions, explain

These problems involve understanding units of length in context and appreciating the sizes of the world records. At the start of the lesson remind children about the notation mm, cm and m and that 10 mm = 1 cm and 100 cm = 1 m.

SUGGESTED QUESTIONS:
- How many mm are the same as 1 cm?
- How could you write this record in millimetres?

Parcel problems: 1 and 2 (pages 23–24)

Processes: reason, make own decisions, explain

These activities provide opportunity for children to determine which calculation is necessary to solve problems involving mass. The problems are varied and require considerable thought and the children should discuss in pairs their thoughts and reasoning. When children are recording number sentences they could be shown how to write each situation using a missing number rather than the last number always being the answer. Some situations may require more than one calculation.

SUGGESTED QUESTIONS:
- How did you find the answer?
- How did you write this as a number sentence or number sentences?
- What method did you use to find the answer?

TV times (page 25)

Processes: reason, explain, record

For this activity, the children should be familiar with the p.m. notation and times written in digital form. Some children may benefit from being given geared clocks to help them work out durations and convert between digital time and analogue time.

SUGGESTED QUESTIONS:
- How many minutes in one hour?
- Can you show me this time on a clock face?
- How many minutes until the next hour?

Represent the information in a puzzle or problem using numbers, images or diagrams; use these to find a solution and present it in context, where appropriate using £.p notation or units of measure

The next theme of the Framework's Using and Applying strand deals with Representing. It focuses on children making sense of a problem or puzzle and organising the information in a way that enables them to solve it. In the early years, children may rely on practical materials and diagrams but as they develop confidence in this area may move on to using numbers, calculations and other modelling, including tables, lists or even the use of algebra.

Triangle tricks (page 26)

Processes: visualise, be systematic, test ideas, trial and improvement

Encourage the children to begin the activity by making different triangles from the shapes and totalling the number of dots on each side. Ask them to record their results and then look at how to swap shapes around so as to have 12 dots on each side.

SUGGESTED QUESTION:
- What strategies did you use?

Question time (page 27)

Processes: explain, reason, record

These questions can be copied onto thin card and laminated and used as a more permanent classroom resource. The cards could be picked at random and used for whole class problem-solving activities in spare moments.

SUGGESTED QUESTIONS:
- How did you find the answer?
- How did you write this as a number sentence or number sentences?

Problem page (page 28)

Processes: reason, explain, record

Observe the methods children use to find the answers, for example noting which children use the picture, their fingers, equipment or a mental method.

- How did you find the answer?
- Which questions did you find the hardest? Why?
- What method did you use to find the answer?
- Did anyone write this as a number sentence?

Match it: 1 and 2 (pages 29–30)

Processes: explain, record, reason

These two sheets provide the children with the opportunity to consider and identify which operations are necessary in solving each question. For these sheets, remind the children that 100p = £1 and 100 cm = 1 m.

SUGGESTED QUESTION:

- Which calculation would you use?

Sweet talk (page 31)

Processes: explain, look for pattern, record, test ideas, trial and improvement, make own decisions

This problem-solving activity requires children to understand the relationship between halving and doubling. Encourage the children to make their own decisions about how to tackle these problems and to record their workings.

SUGGESTED QUESTIONS:

- What was difficult about this task?
- How could you record what you did so that someone else would be able to work it out?

Campsite capers (page 32)

Processes: visualise, make decisions, reason, be systematic, test ideas

Remind the children that they do not necessarily need to work through the clues in order.

SUGGESTED QUESTIONS:

- How did you find this solution?
- Have you checked each rule against your answers?
- If you were to do this again, would you try a different way?

Sheep solutions (page 33)

Processes: visualise, make decisions, reason, be systematic, test ideas

As for the previous activity, remind the children that they do not necessarily need to work through the clues in order.

SUGGESTED QUESTIONS:

- How did you find this solution?
- Have you checked each rule against your answers?

Sensible statements (page 34)

Processes: reason, record, explain

In this activity, the numbers can be changed before copying to

provide further investigations.

SUGGESTED QUESTIONS:

- How could you work this out?
- Why did you decide to record it like this?

Coin quiz (page 35)

Processes: record, explain, reason

This activity provides the children with practice in using pounds/pence notation. Some children may benefit from being given coins to work with. Draw attention to the fact that some questions contain 10p coins and others contain 1p coins.

SUGGESTED QUESTIONS:

- What does £4.02 mean?
- How would you write 3 pounds and eleven pence?

Follow a line of enquiry by deciding what information is important; make and use lists, tables and graphs to organise and interpret the information

This theme encourages children to pursue lines of enquiry. Initially children learn to ask questions and go on to develop skills of planning, organisation and decision-making. Children need to be taught how to use pictures, lists and diagrams when organising information and supporting their line of enquiry.

Flower totals: 1 and 2 (pages 36–37)

Processes: be systematic, make decisions, look for pattern, record, compare

Ensure that children understand the rules for the flower totals investigation, i.e. that each petal must have a number greater than zero and that the total of the petals is the number in the centre. Discuss when flowers are classed as the same, as in the example given.

SUGGESTED QUESTIONS:

- How many different ways did you find?
- How can you be sure that you have found them all?
- Were you systematic?

Dice: 1 and 2 (pages 38–39)

Processes: be systematic, make decisions, look for pattern, record, compare, reason

Encourage the children to compare their solutions and to work systematically to check whether they have found all the possibilities.

SUGGESTED QUESTIONS:

- How many different ways did you find?
- How can you be sure that you have found them all?
- Were you systematic?

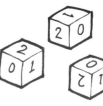

Someone said: 1 and 2 (pages 40–41)

Processes: make decisions, record, co-operate, predict

These activity sheets encourage the children to make decisions and to plan how to follow lines of enquiry by collecting data.

SUGGESTED QUESTION:

- How did you decide what to do?
- What do you think the outcome might be?

Sorting coins (page 42)

Processes: visualise, compare, reason

This activity helps the children to appreciate how Venn diagrams can be used to represent information and how they can be used to show similarities and differences in a clear way. By introducing activities like this, children can begin to realise how such diagrams can be used when they are making and recording their own investigations. Provide sets of coins for children in pairs.

SUGGESTED QUESTIONS:

- Why did you put the 5p coin there?
- Why is the 50p coin outside both those rings?

Lines of enquiry (page 43)

Processes: predict, test ideas, make decisions, trial and improvement, record

As an extension activity, encourage the children to find different ways of recording so that others can follow the instructions and repeat the steps.

SUGGESTED QUESTION:

- How could you show this so that someone else could understand how you solved these problems?

Identify patterns and relationships involving numbers or shapes, and use these to solve problems

Reasoning should go on in all areas of using and applying mathematics. This theme focuses on making deductions based on patterns, properties and relationships. Children should be encouraged to hear and develop the language and vocabulary of reasoning and to use logical steps when reasoning.

Bing, Bong, Bang (page 44)

Processes: be systematic, look for pattern, compare, record, reason

Encourage the children to work systematically. Some children will begin to notice that, to an extent, they can use one set of answers to help them find the next (for example, by swapping over all the Bings with Bongs).

SUGGESTED QUESTIONS:

- What patterns did you use to help you?
- What patterns did you notice?
- How do you know you have found all the solutions?

Find my house (page 45)

Processes: visualise, compare, test ideas, trial and improvement, be systematic, look for pattern

Once the children begin listing solutions they will notice patterns in the cards and realise that by making one substitution each time they will eventually find all the solutions.

SUGGESTED QUESTIONS:

- How would you describe how to get to house number 7?
- How is that set of instructions different from house number 5?

Chair challenge (page 46)

Processes: trial and improvement, test ideas, record, explain, reason

Encourage the children to notice patterns in the numbers, for example to realise that 3 rows of 5 will have the same number of chairs as 5 rows of 3 etc. Encourage them to work systematically.

SUGGESTED QUESTIONS:

- What patterns did you use to help you?
- What patterns did you notice?
- How do you know you have found all the solutions?

Ways to pay (page 47)

Processes: be systematic, compare, reason, record, look for pattern, explain

Encourage the children to describe any systematic strategies they used to help them find further solutions.

SUGGESTED QUESTIONS:

- How many different ways did you find to pay 8p?
- Are those all the ways?
- What is the smallest number of coins you need?
- What patterns do you notice?

Patterns (page 48)

Processes: look for pattern, compare, reason, predict, test ideas, explain

Encourage children to discuss the patterns in the numbers and to say whether it is the tens or units digit changing

each time and which numbers in the calculations are increasing or decreasing.

SUGGESTED QUESTIONS:

- Can you describe this pattern?
- What do you predict?
- How could you check?

Pattern maker (page 49)

Processes: look for pattern, compare, reason, predict, test ideas, explain

There are a wide variety of different patterns that the children could make with these cards. It might be useful to give the children a copy of the previous activity before starting this one to give them ideas about different types of pattern that are possible.

SUGGESTED QUESTIONS:

- Can you describe this pattern?
- What do you predict?
- How could you check?

Miss Moneybags (page 50)

Processes: look for pattern, test ideas, predict, reason

This activity encourages the children to see patterns in numbers that can be used to help them solve problems more quickly. Having completed the sheet, ask the children questions about the number of 10p, 1p or £1 coins that make different amounts. Encourage them to use the patterns they notice to explain how they answered them quickly.

SUGGESTED QUESTION/PROMPT:

- Describe the relationship between the number of £1, 10p and 1p coins in each amount of money.
- How could you use that to help you answer this question?

Right-angle wrangle & Right-angle tangle
(pages 51–52)

Processes: look for pattern, explain, reason, compare, record

Children can work in pairs or small groups to compare and discuss their answers. Ensure the children only count right angles that are inside the shapes, not those outside.

SUGGESTED QUESTIONS:

- Do you know the name of this shape?
- How many right angles has it?
- Do you notice any patterns in the numbers of right angles?

Clock angles (page 53)

Processes: visualise, test ideas, look for pattern, record

These questions can be used as a lead-in to a wider investigation about the number of right angles turned by the minute hand between pairs of times.

SUGGESTED QUESTIONS:

- How can you work out answers quickly?
- What do you notice about these two times?
- How many right angles does the minute hand turn in each hour?

True or false? (page 54)

Processes: look for pattern, test ideas, predict, reason

Ensure the children provide sufficient answers to prove or disprove each statement.

SUGGESTED QUESTIONS:

- What examples can you give me?
- Is this true or false?
- How can you be sure?
- Why?

Describe and explain methods, choices and solutions to puzzles and problems, orally and in writing, using pictures and diagrams

The final theme is Communicating, including both oral and recorded communications. Children should be given opportunities to express their thinking, their reasoning and to communicate their findings to others and also to make personal records of their own. In lessons, children should be encouraged to work with others, discussing decisions to be made, describing actions taken and conclusions made.

Domino distractions: 1 and 2 (pages 55–56)

Processes: look for pattern, reason, test ideas, be systematic

The second Domino sets sheet can be used to provide further opportunities for children to investigate this domino grid.

SUGGESTED QUESTIONS:

- What are the totals?
- Can you explain how you worked this out?

Centi-pods (page 57)

Processes: visualise, reason, trial and improvement, test ideas, compare

As children are investigating this context they may begin to notice patterns in the possibilities. Encourage them to look for reflections and rotations of the same shapes.

SUGGESTED QUESTIONS:

• What other shapes have you found?
• How could you record this for someone else to understand?

Telling stories (page 58)

Processes: explain, reason, ask own questions

This activity encourages the children to think of their own stories to match given calculations. Provide a range of examples and contexts for children to think about before beginning this sheet, for example shopping with money, numbers of sweets, vegetables, pieces of fruit, measurement contexts and so on. Invite the children to read out their stories for others to listen to and ask the other children to guess the calculation. Calculations can be altered before copying.

SUGGESTED QUESTIONS:

• What could your story be about?
• What has to happen?

Noah's arcs (addition and subtraction) (pages 59–60)

Processes: explain, compare, reason

Encourage the children to describe their strategies for working out the answer. Ask them to demonstrate this in different ways, for example using practical material, number lines, 100-squares, place value cards. The numbers can be altered before copying to provide differentiation.

SUGGESTED QUESTIONS:

• What calculation do these arrows represent?
• Which number is missing here?
• Why?
• How can you be sure?
• Do you agree?

Share and share alike (page 61)

Processes: explain, reason, record, compare

This activity encourages the children to describe the strategies they would use to solve these problems and to consider the different ways that this could be done. You could give a time limit for children to make their predictions so that they do not write their calculated answer as a prediction.

Calculations can be altered before copying.

SUGGESTED QUESTIONS:

• What would you do?
• What other ways could it be done?

Broken keys (page 62)

Processes: explain, reason, ask own questions

It is important that children are given the opportunity to consider different ways to answer calculations without using the keys on the calculators marked with a cross.

Possible suggestions are given in the Answers, but children will find their own strategies and these should be discussed together as a class.

SUGGESTED QUESTIONS:

• What would you do?
• Is there another way?

Using the CD-ROM

The CD-ROM included with this book contains an easy-to-use software program that allows you to print out pages from the book, to view them (e.g. on an interactive whiteboard) or to customise the activities to suit the needs of your pupils.

Getting started

It's easy to run the software. Simply insert the CD-ROM into your CD drive and the disk should autorun and launch the interface in your web browser.

If the disk does not autorun, open 'My Computer' and select the CD drive, then open the file 'start.html'.

Please note: this CD-ROM is designed for use on a PC. It will also run on most Apple Macintosh computers in Safari however, due to the differences between Mac and PC fonts, you may experience some unavoidable variations in the typography and page layouts of the activity sheets.

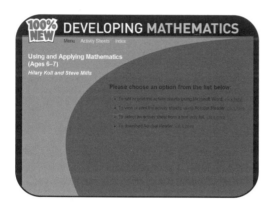

The Menu screen

Four options are available to you from the main menu screen.

The first option takes you to the Activity Sheets screen, where you can choose an activity sheet to edit or print out using Microsoft Word.

(If you do not have the Microsoft Office suite, you might like to consider using OpenOffice instead. This is a multi-platform and multi-lingual office suite, and an 'open-source' project. It is compatible with all other major office suites, and the product is free to download, use and distribute. The homepage for OpenOffice on the Internet is: www.openoffice.org.)

The second option on the main menu screen opens a PDF file of the entire book using Adobe Reader (see below). This format is ideal for printing out copies of the activity sheets or for displaying them, for example on an interactive whiteboard.

The third option allows you to choose a page to edit from a text-only list of the activity sheets, as an alternative to the graphical interface on the Activity Sheets screen.

Adobe Reader is free to download and to use. If it is not already installed on your computer, the fourth link takes you to the download page on the Adobe website.

You can also navigate directly to any of the three screens at any time by using the tabs at the top.

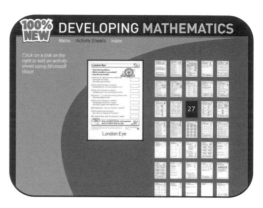

The Activity Sheets screen

This screen shows thumbnails of all the activity sheets in the book. Rolling the mouse over a thumbnail highlights the page number and also brings up a preview image of the page.

Click on the thumbnail to open a version of the page in Microsoft Word (or an equivalent software program, see above.) The full range of editing tools are available to you here to customise the page to suit the needs of your particular pupils. You can print out copies of the page or save a copy of your edited version onto your computer.

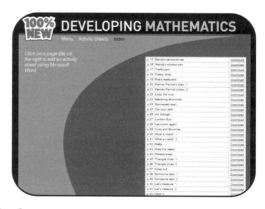

The Index screen

This is a text-only version of the Activity Sheets screen described above. Choose an activity sheet and click on the 'download' link to open a version of the page in Microsoft Word to edit or print out.

Technical support

If you have any questions regarding the *100% New Developing Literacy* or *Developing Mathematics* software, please email us at the address below. We will get back to you as quickly as possible.

educationalsales@acblack.com

Chocolate matters

There are 36 chocolates in a box.
17 are milk chocolate, 6 are white chocolate
and the rest are dark chocolate.

• **Write a calculation for each problem and solve it.**

1 How many in each box are dark chocolate?

2 From a box, how many people can have 5 chocolates each?

3 How many chocolates are there in 3 boxes?

4 James has a whole box. He eats a quarter of them.
How many are left in the box?

5 If you wanted 24 white chocolates, how many boxes
would you need?

6 The Jones family have a box. Tom eats 8, Isobel eats half as
many as Tom and Mum eats 3. How many are left?

NOW TRY THIS!

• **Write** 3 **word problems of your
own about the box of chocolates.**

Teachers' note The numbers can be altered before copying to provide differentiation. Encourage
the children to write each question as a calculation and to describe their strategy for working out
each answer, including showing this on a number line, using a written method or on a 100-square.

*100% New Developing Mathematics
Using and Applying
Mathematics: Ages 7–8*
© A & C BLACK

Fruit corner

- **Answer each question.**
- **Show your working.**

1 6 apples are cut into quarters. How many children can have 3 pieces each?

2 Jo has 3 satsumas. Each satsuma has 12 segments. How many children can have 4 segments each?

3 9 pears are cut in half. How many children can have 3 pieces each?

4 5 peaches are cut into quarters. How many children can have 2 pieces each?

5 A bowl holds 30 grapes. 8 children are given 3 each. How many grapes in the bowl now?

6 3 apples are cut into eighths. How many children can have 3 pieces each?

7 A pineapple is cut into 8 slices. Each slice is cut into 5 chunks. How many chunks altogether?

8 Some bananas are cut into 15 slices each. There are 60 slices altogether. How many bananas?

NOW TRY THIS!

- **Make up 2 fruit questions for a partner to solve.**

Teachers' note The numbers can be altered before copying to provide differentiation. Encourage the children to use pictorial methods or to write each question as a calculation and describe their strategy for working out each answer.

100% New Developing Mathematics Using and Applying Mathematics: Ages 7–8
© A & C BLACK

Two numbers

• **Find the two missing numbers on each card.**

Two numbers 2 5

Their total is 7.
Their product is 10.

Two numbers ☐ ☐

Their total is 5.
Their product is 6.

Two numbers ☐ ☐

Their total is 14.
Their product is 40.

Two numbers ☐ ☐

Their total is 10.
Their product is 25.

Two numbers ☐ ☐

Their total is 12.
Their product is 20.

Two numbers ☐ ☐

Their total is 11.
Their product is 10.

Two numbers ☐ ☐

Their total is 12.
Their product is 35.

Two numbers ☐ ☐

Their total is 19.
Their product is 90.

NOW TRY THIS!

• **Make up 2 of your own for a partner to solve.**

Two numbers ☐ ☐

Their total is ____.
Their product is ____.

Two numbers ☐ ☐

Their total is ____.
Their product is ____.

Teachers' note The children should be reminded of the words 'total' and 'product'. Encourage them to begin to generalise about how to work out the two numbers in each case. Ask them to say what strategies they used to help them work out the two numbers. Did they find the total clue or the product clue most useful initially?

**100% New Developing Mathematics
Using and Applying
Mathematics: Ages 7–8**
© A & C BLACK

Spiders and flies

Here is some information.

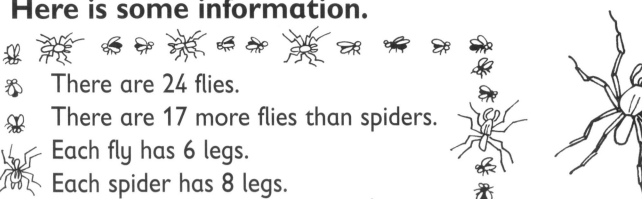

There are 24 flies.

There are 17 more flies than spiders.

Each fly has 6 legs.

Each spider has 8 legs.

• **Write** 4 **questions about the information for a partner to answer. Start your questions with…**

How many…?   How many more…?   How many fewer…?

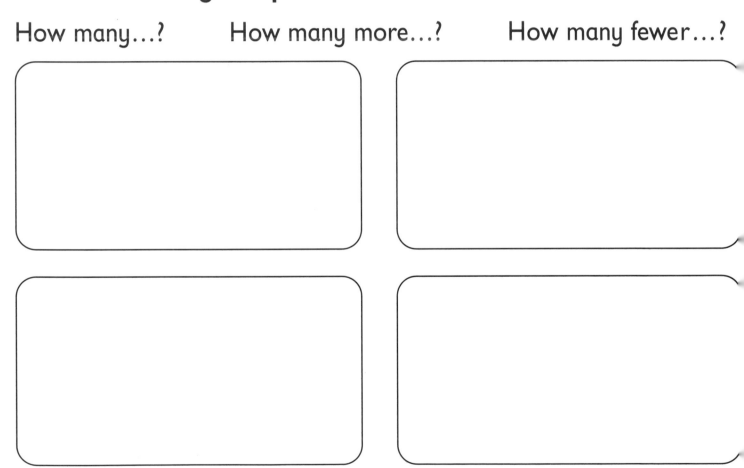

NOW TRY THIS!

• **Swap sheets with a partner and answer their questions.**

Teachers' note This activity encourages children to make up their own questions using appropriate vocabulary. When children exchange sheets for the extension activity, encourage them to describe how they decided what to do and encourage them to use number sentences to show the operation used. Adjust numbers to make them appropriate for the children's abilities.

**100% New Developing Mathematic
Using and Applying
Mathematics: Ages 7–8**
© A & C BLACK

The Street

- **Talk to a partner about how to solve each problem.**

1 36 people live in the street. 4 people live in each house. How many houses are there?

$36 \div 4 = 9$

2 On Monday the postman delivers 3 letters to each house. How many letters does he deliver?

3 Of the 36 people in the street, 17 are children. How many are adults?

4 The houses are numbered 1 to 9. What is the total of all the house numbers?

5 3 houses have 5 windows and 6 houses have 4 windows. How many windows in total?

6 There are 7 lamp-posts on one side of the street and twice as many on the other side. How many lamp-posts altogether?

7 The street lights come on at 7 in the evening and go off at 6 in the morning. How many hours is this?

8 4 houses have 2 cars each and 5 houses have 1 car each. How many cars altogether?

NOW TRY THIS!

- **Make up 2 of your own street questions for a partner to solve.**

Teachers' note Encourage the children to use number sentences to show what they have decided to do for each calculation and ask them to describe their methods for answering each question. They could record their strategies on the back of the sheet.

100% New Developing Mathematics
Using and Applying
Mathematics: Ages 7–8
© A & C BLACK

Pick 3 cards

- **Cut out the cards.**
- **Pick** [2] **small cards and a question card.**
- **Solve the problem.**

How much does it cost for both items?	How much more to buy the more expensive item than the cheaper one?
If you bought the cheaper item, how much change from £5?	If you bought the more expensive item, how much change from £10?
Which is more expensive, 4 of the cheaper item or 2 of the more expensive item?	How much more to buy the more expensive item than the cheaper one?
If you bought both items, how much change from £10?	How much to buy 10 of the cheaper item?
How much to buy 2 of the more expensive item?	How much change from £10 if you buy 2 of the cheaper item?

48p	90p	£2.55
£3.50	£2.99	45p
£2.75	£4.99	£2.45
65p	40p	£1.25
37p	£1.30	£4.50

Teachers' note The cards could be copied onto thin card and laminated as a more practical and durable classroom resource. The prices could be changed before copying to provide differentiated sheets.

100% New Developing Mathematics
Using and Applying
Mathematics: Ages 7–8
© A & C BLACK

At the ice rink

- **Cut out the cards.**
- **What calculations are needed?**
- **How did you decide?**

Work with a partner to solve these problems.

1 Jasmine skated round the rink 26 times and then 7 more times. How many times did she skate round in total?

2 Chloe went to the ice rink 8 times in February and 13 times in March. How many times did she go altogether?

3 Urvi went to the ice rink every day for 3 weeks. How many times did she go to the rink?

4 It costs £3.70 for a child and £5.80 for an adult to go into the ice rink. How much does it cost for 2 children and an adult?

5 Skate hire costs £2.10 for a pair of skates. How much does it cost for 5 pairs of skates?

6 It costs £5.80 for each child to skate (including skate hire). A group of children pay £23.20. How many children are there?

7 It costs £7.90 for each adult to skate (including skate hire). Some adults pay £23.70. How many adults are there?

8 There were 34 people on the ice. 26 come off and 17 more go on. How many are there now?

9 There were 27 people on the ice. 12 more go on and 15 come off. How many are there now?

10 Josh skated round 45 times. This was 8 times fewer than Fay. How many times did Fay skate round?

Teachers' note Some of these problems contain distracting words such as 'times' (as in the second question) or 'more' when multiplication or addition respectively is not the operation required. It is important that children interpret questions correctly rather than looking for trigger words to tell them what to do. They could record their calculations on the back of each card.

100% New Developing Mathematics Using and Applying Mathematics: Ages 7–8 © A & C BLACK

Express pizza

• **Use the menu to help you.**

	small	medium	large
Pan	£4.99	£8.99	£10.49
Italian	£5.99	£10.99	£12.99
Soft crust	£6.49	£11.49	£13.99

* All include 4 toppings of your choice

1 How much for:

a) 2 small Pan pizzas?

£ _____

b) 3 medium Italian pizzas?

£ _____

c) 2 large Soft crust pizzas?

£ _____

d) 1 large and 1 small Pan?

£ _____

e) 3 large Italian pizzas
and 1 small Soft crust?

£ _____

f) 2 medium Soft crust pizzas
and 2 small Italian pizzas?

£ _____

2 How much change from £20 for:

a) 3 small Italian pizzas?

£ _____

b) 1 large Pan pizza?

£ _____

c) 2 medium Pan pizzas?

£ _____

d) 4 small Pan pizzas?

£ _____

NOW TRY THIS!

• **If you have £20, have you enough money to buy 3 small Soft crust pizzas?** _____

Teachers' note Encourage children to round the prices and to work with whole or half pounds and then adjust for the pence when finding totals and giving change. Ask them to record their methods and the calculations they use on the back of the sheet.

**100% New Developing Mathematics
Using and Applying
Mathematics: Ages 7–8
© A & C BLACK**

Loop the loop

* **Cut out the cards.**
* **Answer the 'start' card. Find the answer on one of the other cards. Then answer that question and so on.**
* **Put the cards in a loop on the table.**

Start   **6 kg**

Fi has 360 g of flour. She shares it equally into four bowls. How much in each bowl?

T

---

75 kg

3 tins of beans each weigh 400 g and a tin of ravioli weighs 800 g. How much do the tins weigh altogether?

D

---

68 kg

A bowl and a potato together weigh 500 g. The bowl weighs 100 g more than the potato. How heavy is the bowl?

N

---

10 kg

A bucket weighs 500 g. A 2 kg brick is placed in the bucket. How heavy is it now?

T

$2\frac{1}{2}$ kg

Sally weighs 36 kg. She weighs 39 kg less than her mum. How heavy is her mum?

O

---

90 g

A baby weighed 3 kg. Its mass increased by 500 g a week for two weeks. How much does it weigh now?

R

---

3 kg

A dog weighs 24 kg. The dog is six times heavier than a cat. How heavy is the cat?

E

---

300 g

A dog weighs 6 kg more than a cat. The animals weigh 12 kg altogether. How heavy is the cat?

C

---

4 kg

A brick weighs $2\frac{1}{2}$ kg. What do four bricks weigh?

Y

---

2 kg

Sam is 12 kg lighter than Pete. Sam weighs 56 kg. How heavy is Pete?

A

Teachers' note As a quick way of checking the children's answers, use the letters at the bottom right of each card. If correctly in order they should spell a phrase. Remind the children that 'g' stands for 'grams' and 'kg' stands for 'kilograms'.

100% New Developing Mathematics Using and Applying Mathematics: Ages 7–8 © A & C BLACK

21

Record breakers

• **Read the world records and fill in the missing numbers.**

> The world's longest goldfish measured 47 cm
> from mouth to tail
>
> The longest rabbit ears measured 79 cm
> in a complete span
>
> The world's longest human hair measured 563 cm
>
> The world record for the highest jump by a dog is 173 cm

1 The length of the world's largest goldfish is:

_____ mm

_____ cm less than half a metre.

2 The longest rabbit ears are:

_____ mm

_____ cm less than 1 metre.

3 The world's longest human hair is:

_____ cm longer than 5 metres

_____ cm shorter than 6 metres.

4 The highest jump by a dog is:

_____ cm higher than a metre and a half

_____ cm less than 2 metres.

NOW TRY THIS!

• **Imagine each world record was broken by 4½ cm. Write each new record.**

Teachers' note Remind the children of the equivalents 10 mm = 1 cm and 100 cm = 1 m. Read through the world records together and encourage the children to visualise (or measure out) each length and consider the size in the context given.

**100% New Developing Mathematics
Using and Applying
Mathematics: Ages 7–8
© A & C BLACK**

- **For each question, write a calculation and work out the answer.**

1

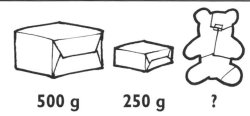

| 500 g | 250 g | ? |

The total mass of these three parcels is 1 kg. What is the mass of the third parcel?

2

The total mass of these three identical parcels is 900 g. What is the mass of each parcel?

3

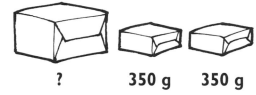

| ? | 350 g | 350 g |

The total mass of these three parcels is 2 kg. What is the mass of the largest parcel?

4

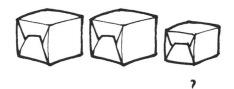

?

Two identical parcels together weigh 900 g. A smaller parcel weighs 100 g less than one of them. What is its mass?

5

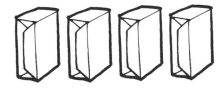

Four identical parcels each weigh 125 g. What is the total mass of the parcels?

6

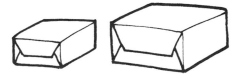

The larger parcel is 3 times heavier than the smaller one. The smaller one weighs 200 g. What is the total mass of the parcels?

Teachers' note As an extension activity, ask the children to make up 2 parcel questions for a partner to solve. The sheets can be given for children to write on in a standard way or alternatively the children could cut out the questions and use as question cards, writing the answers on the back.

**100% New Developing Mathematics
Using and Applying
Mathematics: Ages 7–8
© A & C BLACK**

23

Parcel problems: 2

- **For each question, write a calculation and work out the answer.**

1

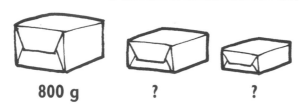

800 g   **?**   **?**

The medium parcel is half the mass of the large one. The smallest is half the mass of the medium one. What is the total mass of the parcels?

2

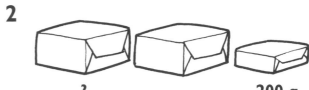

?   **200 g**

The total mass of the parcels is 2 kg. Two have the same mass and the smaller one weighs 200 g. What is the mass of one of the larger ones?

3

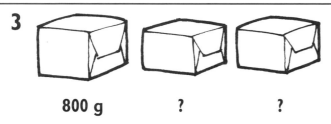

800 g   **?**   **?**

The total mass of the parcels is 2 kg. Two have the same mass and the larger one weighs 800 g. What is the mass of one of the smaller ones?

4

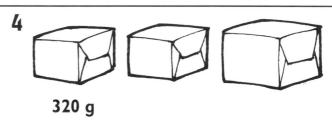

320 g

Two identical parcels each weigh 320 g. A larger parcel weighs 180 g more than one of them. What is the total mass of the parcels?

5

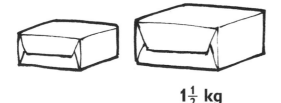

1½ kg

The larger parcel is 3 times heavier than the smaller one. The larger one weighs 1½ kg. What is the total mass of the parcels?

6

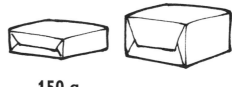

150 g

The larger parcel is 4 times heavier than the smaller one. The smaller one weighs 150 g. What is the mass of the larger parcel?

24

Teachers' note As an extension activity, ask the children to make up 2 parcel questions for a partner to solve. The sheets can be given for children to write on in a standard way or alternatively the children could cut out the questions and use as question cards, writing the answers on the back.

100% New Developing Mathematics
Using and Applying
Mathematics: Ages 7–8
© A & C BLACK

• Use the TV times to help you answer the questions.

Remember to watch:
News - 1:00 p.m.   Watchdog - 7:30 p.m.
Brainy Quiz - 2:45 p.m.   Film - 8:50 p.m.

1 The News runs for 25 minutes.

What time does it end? _____

2 How long after midday does

Brainy Quiz come on? _____

3 Brainy Quiz runs for 30 minutes.

What time does it end? _____

4 Watchdog ends at 7:55 p.m.

How long does the show last? _____

5 Mrs Smith looks at her watch at 8:10 p.m. How long does she

have to wait until the film starts? _____

6 The film runs for 1 hour and 45 minutes.

When does it end? _____

NOW TRY THIS!

• **Write** 3 **questions of your own about the TV times for a partner to solve.**

Teachers' note Read through the TV times together and revise the meaning of p.m. Encourage children to describe their decision making when choosing how to work the answer out. Provide them with geared clocks if necessary. The times can be altered to provide differentiation and variety.

100% New Developing Mathematics Using and Applying Mathematics: Ages 7–8 © A & C BLACK

- **Cut out the pieces. Arrange them to make a large triangle. Each side of the triangle must have** 12 **dots.**

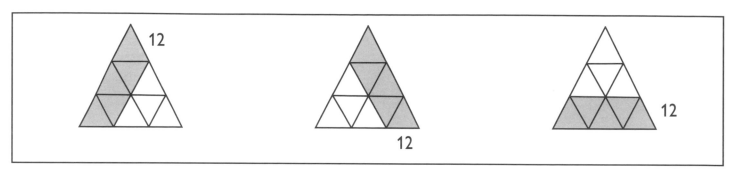

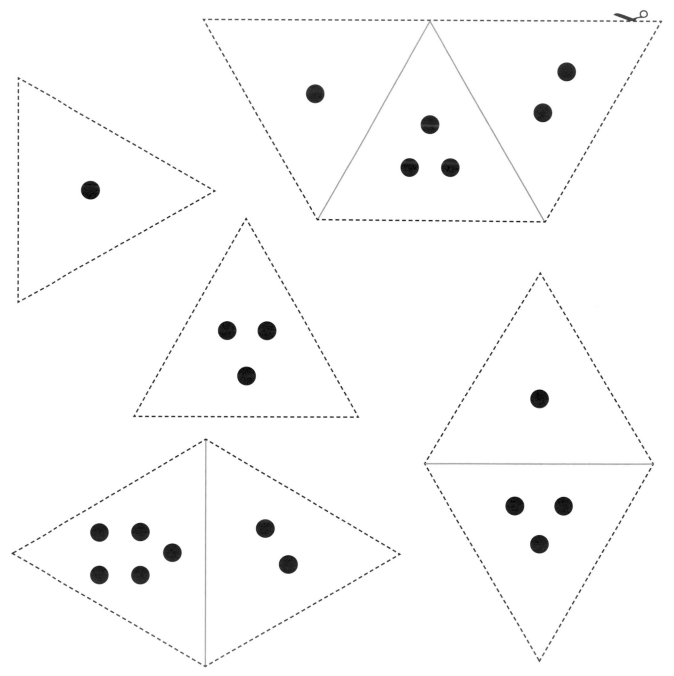

Teachers' note This puzzle requires perseverance and trial and improvement strategies. Note which children use reasoning strategies and those who give up quickly. See page 7 for further hints that can be given to help children find a solution.

**100% New Developing Mathematics
Using and Applying
Mathematics: Ages 7–8**
© A & C BLACK

Question time

- **For each question, write a calculation and work out the answer.**

I think of a number and add 12 to it. My total is 28. What is my number?

I think of a number and subtract it from 40. The answer is 17. What is my number?

I think of a number and multiply it by 3. The product is 18. What is my number?

I think of a number. My number is 24 less than 50. What is my number?

I think of a number and divide it by 5. The answer is 10. What is my number?

I think of a number and subtract 30 from it. The answer is 60. What is my number?

I think of a number. My number is 24 greater than 17. What is my number?

There are 4 of a number in 24. What is the number?

 **NOW TRY THIS!**

- **Make up** $\boxed{2}$ **of your own for a partner to solve.**

Teachers' note Note that different calculations could be written for each question. Ask the children to show how they might solve each question on a number line or 100-square. Encourage them to describe the strategies they used and to compare differences in the calculations suggested for each question, for example [ ] + 12 = 28 or 28 – 12 = [ ].

100% New Developing Mathematics Using and Applying Mathematics: Ages 7–8 © A & C BLACK

27

Problem page

- **Write** | calculations | **for each problem to show how you might work out the answer.**

Work in pairs.

3 drinks cost 24p. What is the cost of 2 drinks? 	4 stickers cost 9p. How many stickers can be bought for 36p? 
Jo bought 10 pencils for 70p. How much would it have cost if she had bought 15 pencils?	4 cakes cost 20p. What is the cost of 5 cakes? 
3 stickers cost 15p. How much would it cost to buy 9 stickers?	A 20p tube of sweets contains 8 sweets. How many sweets could I buy with 60p? 
5 fruit bars cost 25p. How many bars could I buy with 75p? 	3 buns cost 18p. What is the cost of 4 buns?
Sam bought 6 pens for 24p. How much would it cost to buy 9 pens? 	4 stamps cost £1. How many stamps could I buy with £1.50? 

Teachers' note Ask the children to work together in pairs and to discuss how each problem could be solved. Discuss the problems together as a class at the end of the lesson and talk about ways of representing each problem as a calculation.

100% New Developing Mathematics Using and Applying Mathematics: Ages 7–8
© A & C BLACK

- **Work with a partner.**
- **Match each question with a number sentence.**
- **Some number sentences can be used more than once.**

Two tables have a difference in length of 15 cm. The shorter table is 90 cm long. What is the length of the longer table?

A notebook and pencil cost 90p. The pencil cost 15p. How much did the notebook cost?

£90 is shared between some people. Each person gets £15. How many people are there?

A ticket costs 90p. What is the price of 15 tickets?

Ben has 90p. He buys a magazine and is left with 15p. How much did the magazine cost?

Pens come in packs of 15. How many packs would you need to have 90 pens?

90 people travelled to a football match. 15 people went in each minibus. How many minibuses were needed?

A plant that was 15 cm tall grew to be 90 cm. How much had it grown?

$15 \times 90 = [\ ]$

$90 + 15 = [\ ]$

$90 - [\ ] = 15$

$[\ ] - 15 = 90$

$[\ ] \times 15 = 90$

$90 \div [\ ] = 15$

$15 + [\ ] = 90$

$90 \div 15 = [\ ]$

NOW TRY THIS!

- **Make up a new story to match each number sentence.**

Teachers' note More than one possible answer is acceptable in most cases, for example the calculation 15 + [   ] = 90 or 90 – [   ] = 15 could refer to the same situation. Some children may find it easier to work out the answer to help them recognise which number sentence is the correct one.

100% New Developing Mathematics Using and Applying Mathematics: Ages 7–8 © A & C BLACK

Match it: 2

- **Work with a partner.**
- **Match** each question with a number sentence.
- **Some number sentences can be used more than once.**

Two pieces of string are cut from a 1 m ball. One piece is 25 cm long. How long is the other piece if only 8 cm is left on the

Into a fishtank Jo pours 1 litre, then 8 litres and then some more until she has 25 litres. How much more did she add?

Josh shares out £1 equally between 25 people. He then gives each person 8p more. How much do they each have now?

Tickets cost £1. Sam buys 8 and pays a 25p booking charge. How much does he pay?

Al has a 1 metre plank of wood. He saws it into 25 cm lengths. How many 1 m planks does he need to have 8 pieces like this?

Beth is given £1 each week for 8 weeks. How many 25p stickers can she buy with the money?

A milkshake is made from 1 egg-cup of juice and 8 egg-cups of milk. Li makes 25 milkshakes. How many egg-cups of drink is this altogether?

A tree that was 1 m tall grew to be 8 times taller. It then grew a further 25 cm. How tall is it now?

$1 + 25 + 8 = [\ \ ]$

$100 - 25 - [\ \ ] = 8$

$100 \div 25 \times [\ \ ] = 8$

$(1 + 8) \times 25 = [\ \ ]$

$100 \times 8 \div 25 = [\ \ ]$

$(100 \times 8) + 25 = [\ \ ]$

$1 + 8 + [\ \ ] = 25$

$(100 \div 25) + 8 = [\ \ ]$

NOW TRY THIS!

- **Make up a story to match this number sentence.**

$100 + [\ \ ] - 25 = 8$

Teachers' note The questions are two-step calculations and children should work together in pairs to discuss them. Some children may find it easier to work out the answer to help them recognise which number sentence is the correct one.

100% New Developing Mathematics
Using and Applying
Mathematics: Ages 7–8
© A & C BLACK

Sweet talk

There were some sweets in a bowl.

☆ First, Andy ate ⬚half⬚ the sweets.

☆ Then Mandy ate ⬚half⬚ the sweets that were left.

☆ Finally, Sandy ate ⬚half⬚ the sweets that were left after Mandy had had hers.

☆ ⬚5⬚ sweets were left in the bowl at the end.

• **How many sweets were in the bowl at the start?**
• **Show your working here.**

NOW TRY THIS!

• **Can you solve this problem in a similar way?**

☆ First, Andy ate ⬚half⬚ the sweets in a bowl.

☆ Then Mandy ate ⬚half⬚ the sweets left.

☆ Finally, Sandy ate a ⬚quarter⬚ of the sweets left.

☆ ⬚3⬚ sweets were left in the bowl at the end.

• **How many sweets were in the bowl at the start?** _____

Teachers' note Ensure that children understand the problem and encourage them to show their working in the box, whether pictorial or numerical. Numbers can be changed before copying, for example change the final 'half' to a 'a third of' and make the final number an even number.

100% New Developing Mathematics Using and Applying Mathematics: Ages 7–8 © A & C BLACK

Campsite capers

- **Work with a partner.**
- **Use the clues to help you work out the** boxed:total **number of children in the tents.**

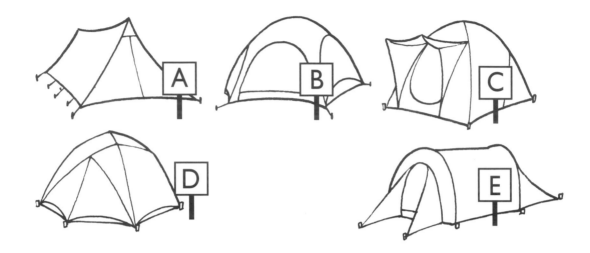

In Tent B there are 3 more children than in tent E.

Tent D has the most children in.
It has 1 more child than in any other tent.

In Tent C there are 2 fewer children than in tent A.

In Tents A and E there are the same number of children.

In Tent B there are 6 children.

- **How many children are at the camp** boxed:altogether **?**

NOW TRY THIS!

- **Draw** 5 **tents of your own and decide how many children are in each. Make up clues for a partner.**

Teachers' note For the extension activity encourage the children to check whether they have given a clue for each tent, without saying how many are in most of the tents. Write up sentences like 'more than', 'fewer than', 'the most', 'the fewest' and 'the same number' on the board to help them make up their own clues.

100% New Developing Mathematic
Using and Applying
Mathematics: Ages 7–8
© A & C BLACK

Sheep solutions

- **Work with a partner. In each barn are ewes and lambs.**
- **Use the clues to help you work out the** total **number of sheep in the barns.**

 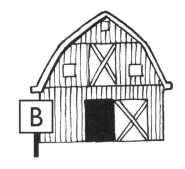 

In Barn A there are 3 more lambs than ewes.

Barn C has 4 lambs and some ewes.

Barn B has the same number of ewes as Barn C.

In Barn C there are 7 sheep altogether.

In Barn B there are 2 lambs.

In Barn A there is 1 ewe.

- **How many sheep are in the barns** altogether **?**
- **How many are: lambs?** ⬚ **ewes?** ⬚

NOW TRY THIS!

- **Draw** 3 **barns of your own and decide how many ewes and lambs are in each. Make up clues for a partner.**

Teachers' note For the extension activity encourage children to check whether they have given a clue for each barn, without saying how many lambs or ewes are in most of the barns. Write up sentences like 'more than', 'fewer than', 'the most', 'the fewest' and 'the same number' on the board to help them make up their own clues.

100% New Developing Mathematics Using and Applying Mathematics: Ages 7–8 © A & C BLACK

Sensible statements

- **Tick** ✔ **the most sensible number sentence for each problem.**

1 There were 40 avocados in a shop. Sam sold some of them and then had 15 left. How many did he sell?

$\diamond - 15 = 40$ $15 - \diamond = 40$ $\diamond - 40 = 15$ $40 - \diamond = 15$

2 There are 42 cakes arranged on some plates. Each plate has 14 cakes on it. How many plates?

$\diamond \div 14 = 42$ $42 \times \diamond = 14$ $\diamond \div 14 = 42$ $42 \div 14 = \diamond$

3 Each packet holds 24 biscuits. Clive buys 3 packets of biscuits. How many biscuits?

$\diamond \times 3 = 24$ $24 \div \diamond = 3$ $24 \times 3 = \diamond$ $\diamond \times 3 = 24$

4 There were some peaches in a shop. Sam sold 14 of them and had 11 left. How many were there at the start?

$14 - \diamond = 11$ $\diamond - 14 = 11$ $11 - 14 = \diamond$ $14 - 11 = \diamond$

NOW TRY THIS!

- **Write** number sentences **to match these problems.**

  3 melons cost 90p. How much do 5 melons cost?

  5 apples cost 35p. How much do 12 apples cost?

Teachers' note Remind children that the focus is not on solving the problem, but rather on deciding which number sentence represents the situation. Encourage the children to describe their reasoning and to make up problems like these of their own.

100% New Developing Mathematic Using and Applying Mathematics: Ages 7–8 © A & C BLACK

Coin quiz

• Move along the track. Work out the total amount of money and find it below. Write the matching letter.

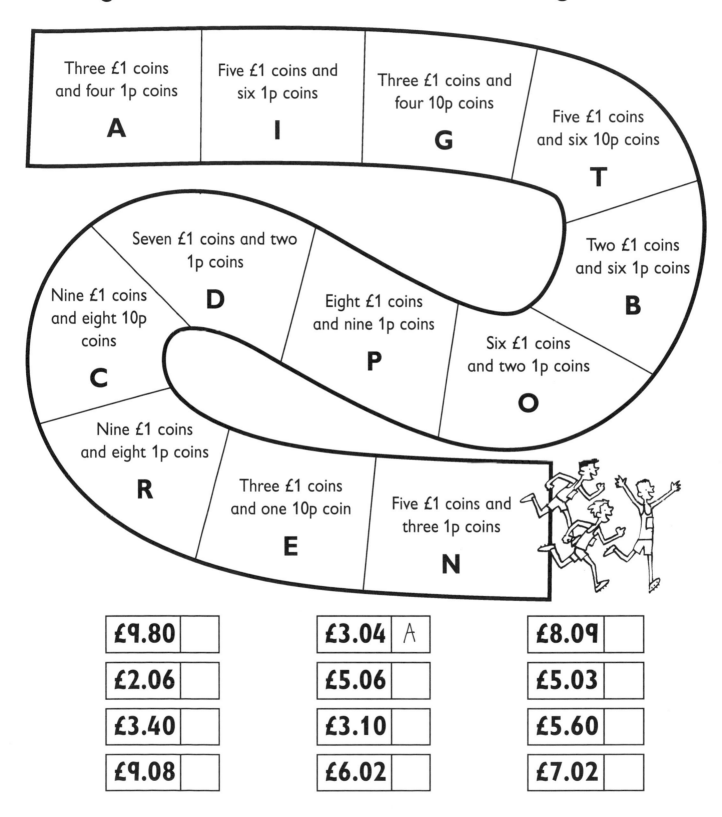

Three £1 coins and four 1p coins
A

Five £1 coins and six 1p coins
I

Three £1 coins and four 10p coins
G

Five £1 coins and six 10p coins
T

Two £1 coins and six 1p coins
B

Seven £1 coins and two 1p coins
D

Eight £1 coins and nine 1p coins
P

Nine £1 coins and eight 10p coins
C

Six £1 coins and two 1p coins
O

Nine £1 coins and eight 1p coins
R

Three £1 coins and one 10p coin
E

Five £1 coins and three 1p coins
N

£9.80	£3.04 A	£8.09
£2.06	£5.06	£5.03
£3.40	£3.10	£5.60
£9.08	£6.02	£7.02

• **What words are spelt in each line?** _____

Teachers' note Draw children's attention to the fact that some contain 10p coins and others 1p coins. Discuss the pounds/pence notation and encourage the children to say the total amounts in words.

100% New Developing Mathematics
Using and Applying
Mathematics: Ages 7–8
© A & C BLACK

35

Flower totals: 1

The | total | of the petal numbers must make the centre number
These two flowers are the **same**…

- **Can you see why?**

Every petal must show a whole number greater than zero.

- **How many** | different | **possible ways are there to make the**
  total | 8 | **?**

NOW TRY THIS! • **What about the total** | 9 | **?**

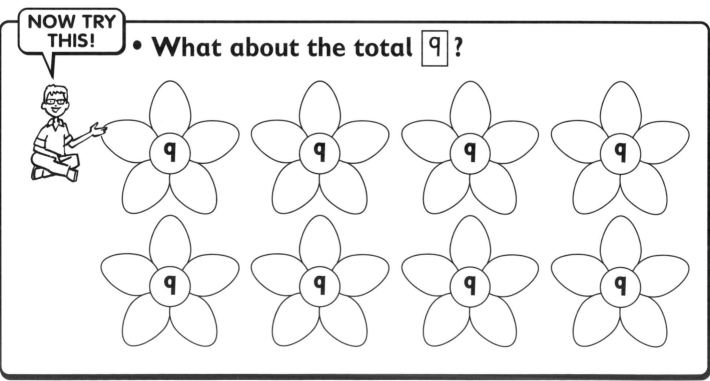

Teachers' note Stress that the number zero cannot be used. The following sheet can be used to investigate other totals between 5 and 12. Encourage the children to generalise and look for patterns in the numbers of possible different ways there are for each number. See page 8 for more information about the patterns.

100% New Developing Mathematic
Using and Applying
Mathematics: Ages 7–8
© A & C BLACK

Teachers' note Use this sheet in conjunction with the previous page for investigating different possible totals. See page 8 for more information. Numbers can be written into the centres of the flowers before copying or given blank for children to investigate their own numbers.

100% New Developing Mathematics Using and Applying Mathematics: Ages 7–8
© A & C BLACK

Dice: 1

- ## You need the nets on 'Dice: 2' to make 3 dice.

  ☆ Roll the 3 dice and find the total.

  ☆ Repeat this 20 times, recording the totals.

  ☆ What do you notice?

- ## What are all the possible │totals│ that can be made with the 3 dice labelled 0, 1 and 2?

[0] + [0] + [0] = 0   [0] + [0] + [1] = 1

[   ] + [   ] + [   ] =   [   ] + [   ] + [   ] =

[   ] + [   ] + [   ] =   [   ] + [   ] + [   ] =

[   ] + [   ] + [   ] =   [   ] + [   ] + [   ] =

[   ] + [   ] + [   ] =   [   ] + [   ] + [   ] =

[   ] + [   ] + [   ] =   [   ] + [   ] + [   ] =

[   ] + [   ] + [   ] =   [   ] + [   ] + [   ] =

[   ] + [   ] + [   ] =   [   ] + [   ] + [   ] =

[   ] + [   ] + [   ] =   [   ] + [   ] + [   ] =

[   ] + [   ] + [   ] =   [   ] + [   ] + [   ] =

[   ] + [   ] + [   ] =   [   ] + [   ] + [   ] =

[   ] + [   ] + [   ] =   [   ] + [   ] + [   ] =

[   ] + [   ] + [   ] =   [   ] + [   ] + [   ] =

NOW TRY THIS!

- ## Use 2 real dice. Write all the possible totals that can be made. Draw a table to help you find all the totals.

Teachers' note When the children are writing the possible totals, encourage them to work systematically. Discuss whether 0+1+0 is classed as the same as 1+0+0 or 0+0+1 and encourage children to reason for themselves. For the extension activity demonstrate how a table can be used to find the 36 different totals. See page 8 for more information.

100% New Developing Mathematics
Using and Applying
Mathematics: Ages 7–8
© A & C BLACK

- **Cut out the dice nets and make 3 dice.**

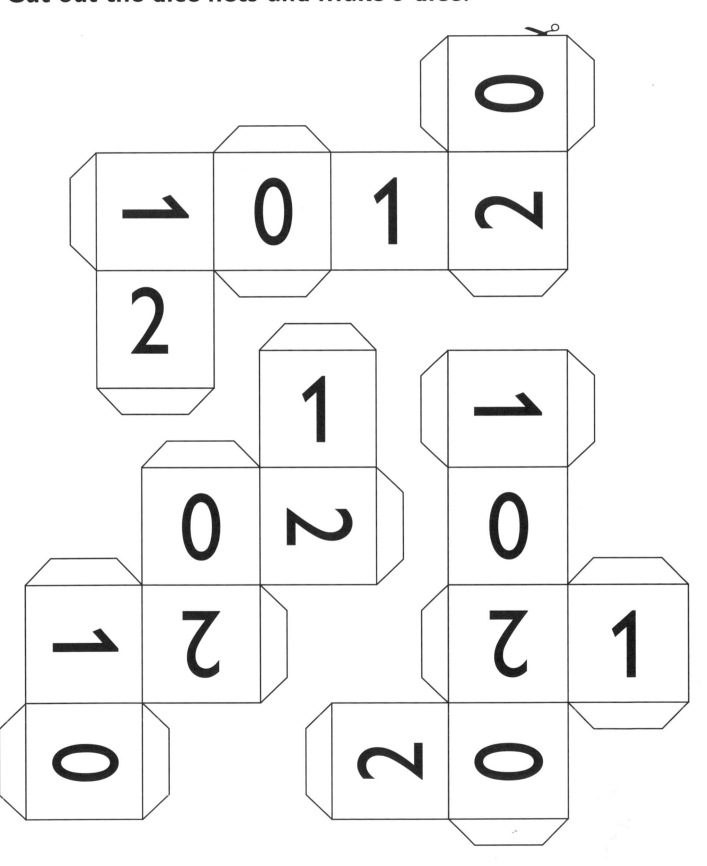

Teachers' note Use this sheet in conjunction with page 38. The sheet should be copied onto card, and the children will need scissors and glue or sticky tape.

**100% New Developing Mathematics
Using and Applying
Mathematics: Ages 7–8
© A & C BLACK**

- **Work with a partner.**
- **Read through the questions and choose one of them to work with.**
- **You will need a copy of 'Someone said: 2'.**

Someone said that more than half the children in our class bring an apple to school.

Is this true?

Someone said that fewer than half the children in our class have one brother.

Is this true?

Someone said that about half the children in our class have the letter 'e' in their name.

Is this true?

Someone said that more than half the children in our class have a shoe size larger than 12.

Is this true?

Someone said that fewer than half the children in our class walk to school.

Is this true?

Someone said that more than half the children in our class go to bed by 9 o'clock.

Is this true?

- **Cut out your chosen question and stick it onto the 'Someone said: 2' activity sheet.**

40

Teachers' note This activity should be done in pairs. The children should choose a question from this sheet and stick it on to page 41. They should then plan how they would go about answering the question. The focus should be on planning the investigation and time should be spent discussing all the children's work.

100% New Developing Mathematics
Using and Applying
Mathematics: Ages 7–8
© A & C BLACK

Someone said: 2

- **Write your names.**

  _____

  _____

- **Show how you could find out whether your statement is** boxed{true} **.**

Stick your chosen question here.

What information we need:

How we would collect it:

What we think we will find and why:

How we would show the information:

100% New Developing Mathematics
Using and Applying
Mathematics: Ages 7–8
© A & C BLACK

41

Sorting coins

- ## Use a full set of coins.
- ## Write where each coin would go in each | Venn | diagram.

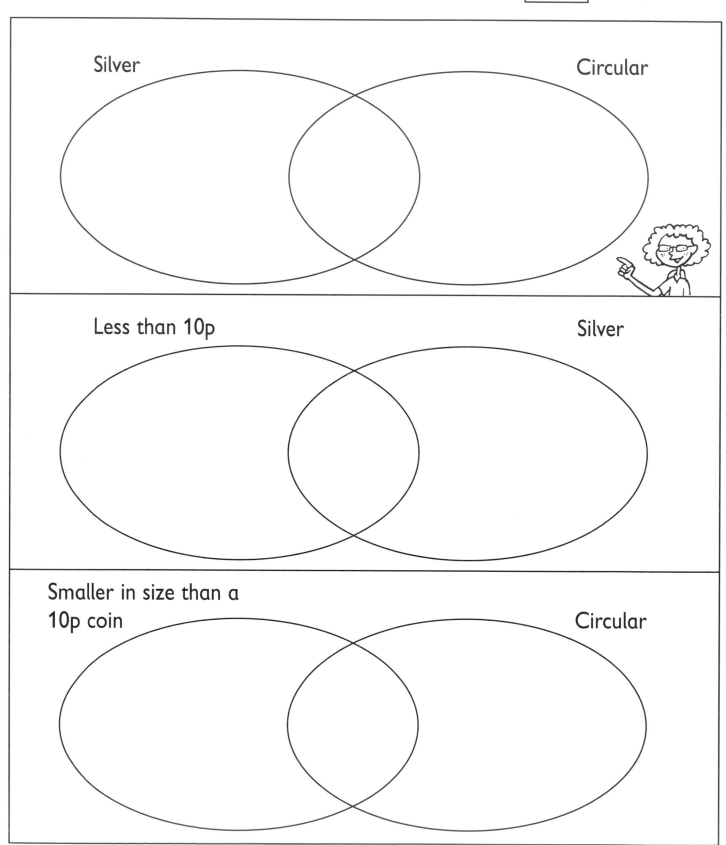

Silver

Circular

Less than 10p

Silver

Smaller in size than a
10p coin

Circular

Teachers' note Provide the children with a £2, £1, 50p, 20p, 10p, 5p, 2p and 1p coin. Encourage them to compare the diagrams and to explain their decisions made when sorting the coins. As an extension activity, the children could draw their own Venn diagram and choose new labels or a different combination of labels than those here.

100% New Developing Mathematics
Using and Applying
Mathematics: Ages 7–8
© A & C BLACK

Lines of enquiry

- **Cut out the cards.**
- **Investigate the problem and find a solution.**
- **Explain to the rest of the class what you did and how you found the answer.**

What is the largest odd number that can be made by multiplying the numbers on two dice?

What is the largest remainder you can have when you divide a number by 4?

What is the total of the first five multiples of 3?

What is the smallest even number that is in the five- and the three-times tables?

What is the largest remainder you can have when you divide a number by 3?

When counting on in fours from zero, what is the first multiple of 10 you reach?

What is the total of the first five multiples of 4?

What is the smallest odd number that is in the five- and the seven-times tables?

What is the largest odd number that can be made by adding the numbers on three dice?

What is the largest number that divides into 24 that is not a multiple of 3?

Teachers' note These cards could be copied onto thin card and laminated for a more permanent classroom resource. The children could be given specific cards or be allowed to choose their own to investigate. They could write explanations of their investigation in the form of a leaflet or poster for others to understand.

100% New Developing Mathematics
Using and Applying
Mathematics: Ages 7–8
© A & C BLACK

Bing, Bong, Bang

- **The words Bing, Bong and Bang can be said in different orders. Write them here.**

Bong Bing Bang

_____

_____   _____

_____   _____

- **Use the words Bing, Bang, Bong, Bung.**
- **Find all the different ways that the words can be said.**

1 Start with Bing.

Bing _____   Bing _____

Bing _____   Bing _____

Bing _____   Bing _____

2 Start with Bong.

Bong _____   Bong _____

Bong _____   Bong _____

Bong _____   Bong _____

3 Start with Bang.

Bang _____   Bang _____

Bang _____   Bang _____

Bang _____   Bang _____

4 Start with Bung.

Bung _____   Bung _____

Bung _____   Bung _____

Bung _____   Bung _____

Teachers' note This activity encourages the children to tackle an investigation systematically, by asking them to work starting with each word in turn. The Spike Milligan poem 'On the Ning, Nang, Nong' could be used as an introduction to this activity.

44

100% New Developing Mathematics
Using and Applying
Mathematics: Ages 7–8
© A & C BLACK

Find my house

- **Cut out the cards below.**
- **Pick an A card, a B card and a C card.**
- **Find which house you reach.**
- **Record your route and house number on paper.**
- **Try this several times. Can every house be reached?**

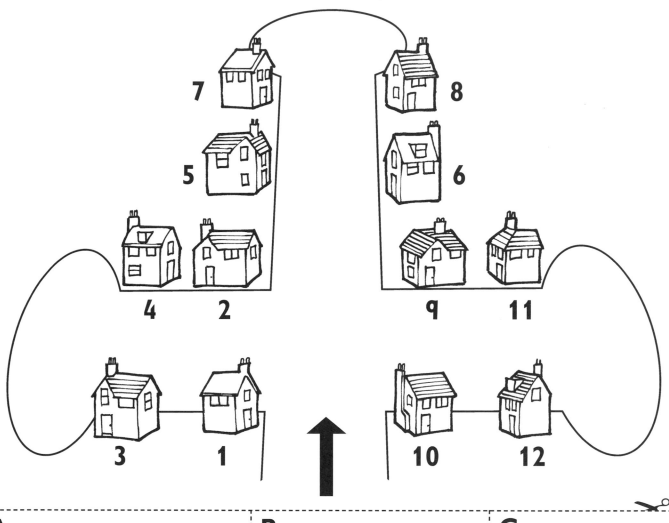

A		B		C	
Turn right					
		first house		on the right	
Turn left					
		second house		on the left	
Go straight on					

Teachers' note Once the children have begun to investigate the combinations of cards, explain that you would like them to record their findings and results as a poster for someone else to understand. This encourages children to be systematic and to consider how best to show the different combinations of cards and the related house numbers.

100% New Developing Mathematics Using and Applying Mathematics: Ages 7–8 © A & C BLACK

Chair challenge

- **Cut out the** number cards **and place them in the boxes.**
- **How many different questions and answers can you find?**

Chairs are arranged in ☐ rows with ☐ chairs in each row. People arrive and sit on the chairs. There are ☐ empty chairs. How many people are there?

- **Write your calculations and answers here.**

NOW TRY THIS!

- **How many more answers are possible if you also had a 7 card?**

5 | 3 | 6 | 4

Teachers' note Encourage the children to notice patterns in the numbers, for example to realise that 3 rows of 5 will have the same number of chairs as 5 rows of 3 etc. Encourage children to work systematically.

100% New Developing Mathematics
Using and Applying
Mathematics: Ages 7–8
© A & C BLACK

Ways to pay

- **Write different ways to pay each amount below.**
- **Then write the** fewest **number of coins needed to pay.**

		Fewest number of coins needed
1p	1p	1 coin
2p	2p or 1p + 1p	1 coin
3p	2p + 1p or 1p + 1p + 1p	2 coins
4p		
5p		
6p		
7p		
8p		
9p		
10p		
11p		
12p		
13p		
14p		
15p		
16p		
17p		
18p		
19p		
20p		

NOW TRY THIS!

- **Which amounts between** 20p **and** 40p **cannot be bought with 3 or fewer coins?**

Teachers' note Encourage children to look for patterns in the numbers and to make predictions about larger amounts. They could group the amounts between 1p and 20p into groups according to the fewest coins needed. See page 9 for more information. Children could ask their own questions like that in the extension activity and investigate amounts further.

100% New Developing Mathematics Using and Applying Mathematics: Ages 7–8 © A & C BLACK

Patterns

• **Fill in the missing digits to continue the patterns.**

4 7 + ☐ 8 = 5 5
3 7 + 1 8 = 5 5
☐ ☐ + 2 8 = 5 5
☐ ☐ + ☐ ☐ = 5 5
☐ ☐ + ☐ ☐ = ☐ ☐

1 5 + 1 9 = 3 4
1 5 + 2 9 = 4 4
1 5 + ☐ ☐ = 5 4
☐ ☐ + ☐ ☐ = ☐ ☐
☐ ☐ + ☐ ☐ = ☐ ☐

☐ 7 + 3 5 = 4 2
1 7 + 3 5 = 5 2
2 7 + 3 5 = 6 2
☐ ☐ + ☐ ☐ = ☐ ☐
☐ ☐ + ☐ ☐ = ☐ ☐

3 0 + 5 2 = 8 2
2 9 + 5 2 = 8 1
2 8 + 5 2 = 8 0
☐ ☐ + ☐ ☐ = ☐ ☐
☐ ☐ + ☐ ☐ = ☐ ☐

8 5 + ☐ 8 = 9 3
7 5 + 1 8 = 9 3
6 5 + 2 8 = 9 3
☐ ☐ + ☐ ☐ = 9 3
☐ ☐ + ☐ ☐ = ☐ ☐

☐ 7 + ☐ 7 = 1 4
1 7 + 1 7 = 3 4
2 7 + 2 7 = 5 4
☐ ☐ + ☐ ☐ = ☐ ☐
☐ ☐ + ☐ ☐ = ☐ ☐

NOW TRY THIS!

• **Talk to a partner about the patterns above.**

Teachers' note Encourage children to discuss the patterns in the numbers and to say whether it is the tens or units digit changing each time and which numbers in the calculations are increasing or decreasing.

**100% New Developing Mathematic
Using and Applying
Mathematics: Ages 7–8
© A & C BLACK**

Pattern maker

- **Cut out the cards. Pick cards to make patterns with. Stick them onto paper and write the answers. If you need other numbers, write them onto the** blank **cards.**

600 + 50 + 7	600 + 40 + 17	600 + 30 + 27
600 + 10 + 47	600 + 20 + 37	700 + 50 + 17
800 + 50 + 7	900 + 50 + 7	600 + 30 + 7
600 + 30 + 17	600 + 30 + 37	600 + 30 + 47
500 + 10 + 47	400 + 10 + 47	300 + 10 + 47
200 + 10 + 47	100 + 10 + 47	900 + 40 + 7
900 + 30 + 7	900 + 20 + 7	900 + 10 + 7
700 + 40 + 27	700 + 30 + 37	700 + 20 + 47
700 + 10 + 57	300 + 10 + 57	300 + 20 + 47
300 + 30 + 37	300 + 40 + 27	300 + 50 + 17

Teachers' note This activity encourages the children to begin to realise how numbers can be partitioned into multiples of 100, tens and ones in different ways. If they are experiencing difficulty in sorting the cards into sets, ask them to take each card in turn and find the total. The cards can then be grouped according to totals and then each set arranged to show partition patterns.

**100% New Developing Mathematics
Using and Applying
Mathematics: Ages 7–8
© A & C BLACK**

49

Miss Moneybags

- **Complete this table to show how many of each coin makes the amount in the bag.**

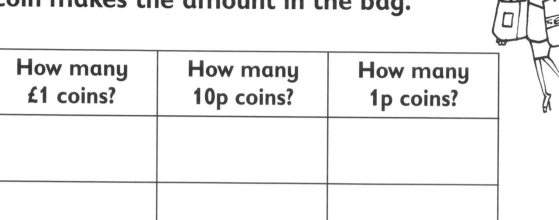

	How many £1 coins?	How many 10p coins?	How many 1p coins?
£2			
£4			
£5			
£8			
£9			
£11			

- **Explain what you notice about the number of £1, 10p and 1p coins.** _____

_____

_____

NOW TRY THIS!

- **Draw another table to show how many £2, 20p and 2p coins make £4, £6, £10 and £12.**

Teachers' note This activity encourages the children to see patterns in numbers that can be used to help them solve problems more quickly. Having completed the sheet, ask the children oral questions about the number of 10p, 1p or £1 coins that make different amounts. Encourage them to use the patterns they notice to explain how they answered them quickly.

100% New Developing Mathematics Using and Applying Mathematics: Ages 7–8 © A & C BLACK

Right-angle wrangle

Tim has ⊡8⊡ identical right-angled triangles.
The other ⊡2⊡ angles in each
triangle are half right angles.

Tim fits them together, adding an extra triangle each time.

• Write what shapes are made and say how many right
  angles each **whole** shape has.

1
    triangle
    I right angle

5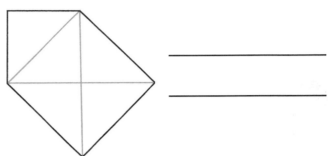

2

6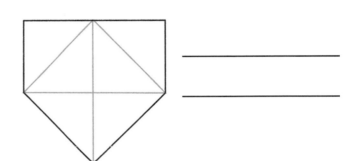

3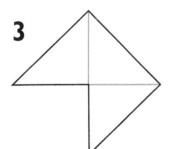

7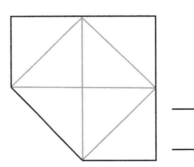

4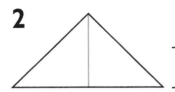

8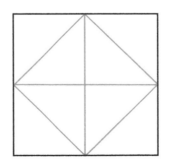

Teachers' note Children could investigate their own shapes formed using identical tiles of a different shape. Remind them that they should only count the right angles that are formed INSIDE each shape and not those that are outside the shape. They could also use page 52 as an extension. Ask the children to mark each right angle on the shapes.

**100% New Developing Mathematics
Using and Applying
Mathematics: Ages 7–8
© A & C BLACK**

Right-angle tangle

Tim has ⊡ 8 identical pentagons.
Three angles are right angles.
Tim fits them together, adding an extra pentagon each time.

• Write how many sides and how many right angles each <u>whole</u> shape has.

1

5 sides

3 right angles

5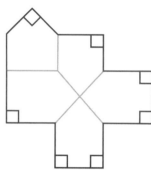

12 sides

7 right angles

2

_____

_____

6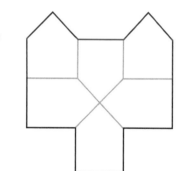

_____

_____

3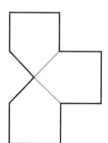

_____

_____

7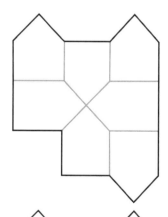

_____

_____

4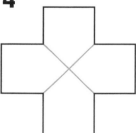

_____

_____

8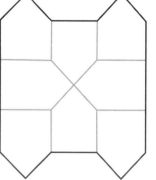

_____

_____

Teachers' note Ask the children to mark each right angle on the shapes. Remind them that they should only count the right angles that are formed INSIDE each shape and not those that are outside the shape. Children could investigate their own shapes formed using identical tiles of a different shape.

**100% New Developing Mathematics
Using and Applying
Mathematics: Ages 7–8**
© A & C BLACK

• **Through how many right angles does the minute hand turn between the times on the clocks in each pair?**

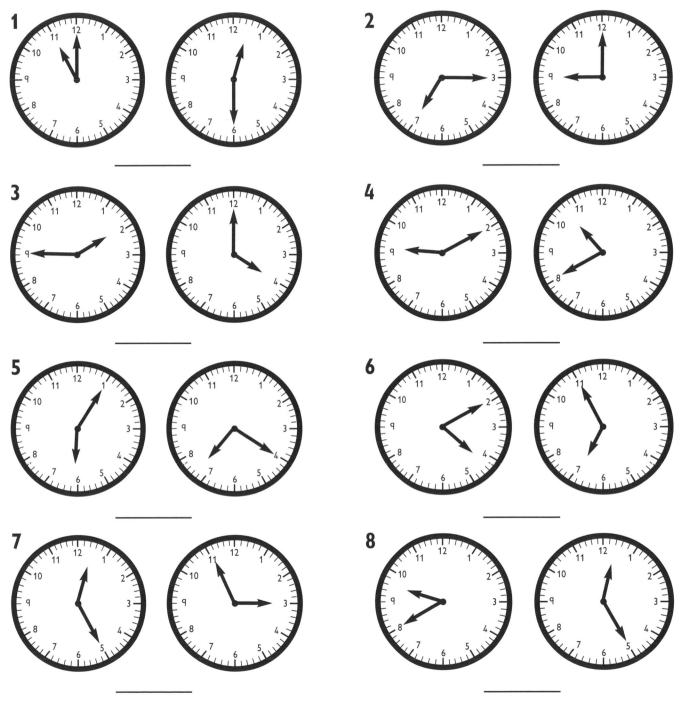

1

2

3

4

5

6

7

8

NOW TRY THIS!

• **Write different pairs of times in the afternoon where the minute hand goes through 11 right angles.**

Teachers' note Remind children that the minute hand is the longer hand and that it turns through 4 right angles in each hour. Also that it passes through a right angle when it moves between say the 2 and the 5. The hands on the clocks can be changed to create a variety of different question banks. For the extension activity, encourage the children to work systematically to write pairs of times.

100% New Developing Mathematics **Using and Applying Mathematics: Ages 7–8** © A & C BLACK

53

True or false?

- Is the statement true or false?
- Colour the correct answer.
- Write examples to show whether it is true or false.

---

1 There are exactly 5 multiples of 3 between 20 and 30.

_____

_____

true

false

---

2 There are exactly 6 multiples of 4 between 30 and 59.

_____

_____

true

false

---

3 If you divide any even number by an even number the answer is always even.

_____

_____

true

false

---

4 If you double any odd number the answer is always even.

_____

_____

true

false

---

5 There are exactly 11 multiples of 5 between 43 and 97.

_____

_____

true

false

---

6 There are exactly 5 multiples of 3 between 26 and 40.

_____

_____

true

false

NOW TRY THIS!

- Write two statements of your own and find out whether they are true or false.

Teachers' note Ask the children to make predictions before checking and finding examples to show whether the statement is true or false. As a further extension activity, the children could amend the statements to make them true.

100% New Developing Mathematics
Using and Applying
Mathematics: Ages 7–8
© A & C BLACK

- **Cut out the dominoes at the bottom of the sheet.**
- **Arrange the dominoes so that the totals along each side are the same.**

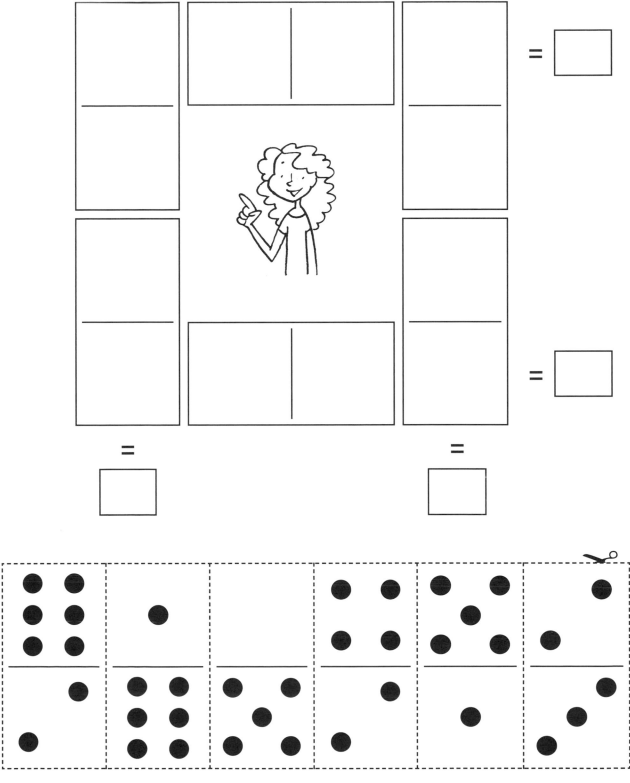

Teachers' note Ask the children to compare their answers and to find out whether there is more than one solution. Other sets of six dominoes, such as those on the following page, can be provided for further experience of this type.

100% New Developing Mathematics Using and Applying Mathematics: Ages 7–8
© A & C BLACK

Domino distractions: 2

- ## Use each set to solve the problem.

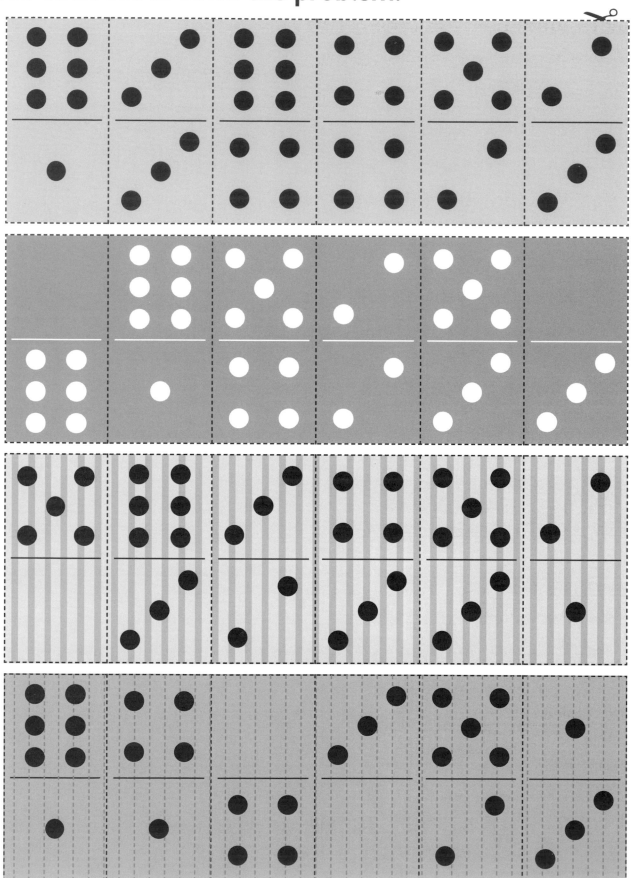

Teachers' note Use in conjunction with page 55.

100% New Developing Mathematics
Using and Applying
Mathematics: Ages 7–8
© A & C BLACK

Centi-pods

A centi-pod is a strange creature that grows $\boxed{1\ cm}$ each year of its life. Each section of its body is a straight line that is $\boxed{1\ cm}$ long.

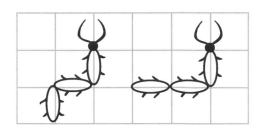

These are 3 years old

Investigate different aged centi-pods.

- **How many different 2-year-old centi-pods can you draw? Then try 3-year-old ones and so on.**

NOW TRY THIS!

- **Make a poster about all the things you have discovered about the centi-pods.**
- **Organise the poster clearly so that others can see what you found out.**

Teachers' note Explain that the bodies of centi-pods hinge at the end of each straight section and can bend to 90° (i.e. they can only be drawn along the grid lines of the squared paper). Urge children to observe when centi-pods are the same but rotated or reflected. Provide plain and squared paper for the extension activity. Ask the children to present their findings clearly using diagrams and words.

100% New Developing Mathematics Using and Applying Mathematics: Ages 7–8 © A & C BLACK

Telling stories

- **Make up a story for each calculation.**
- **Choose one of these units to use in each story:**

kg	£	m	p	cm	ml

20 + 5 – 7

_____

_____

_____

_____

32 – 21 + 4

_____

_____

_____

_____

(4 × 5) + 3

_____

_____

_____

_____

(24 ÷ 3) + 2

_____

_____

_____

_____

(100 ÷ 4) – 20

_____

_____

_____

_____

(10 × 6) – 9

_____

_____

_____

_____

NOW TRY THIS!

- **Write the answer to each calculation, giving the correct unit used in each story.**

Teachers' note Provide a range of examples and contexts for children to think about before beginning this sheet, for example shopping with money, numbers of sweets, vegetables, pieces of fruit, measurement contexts and so on. Invite children to read out their stories for others to listen to and ask the other children to guess the calculation. Calculations can be altered before copying.

100% New Developing Mathematics
Using and Applying
Mathematics: Ages 7–8
© A & C BLACK

Noah's arcs (addition)

- Fill in the missing numbers on each diagram to show how Noah answered each question.

| 38 + 7 |

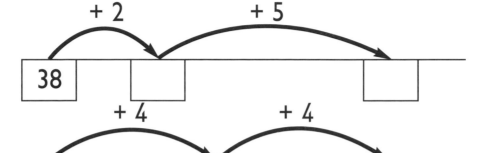

+ 2   + 5

38 ☐ ☐

| 46 + 8 |

+ 4   + 4

46 ☐ ☐

| 65 + 7 |

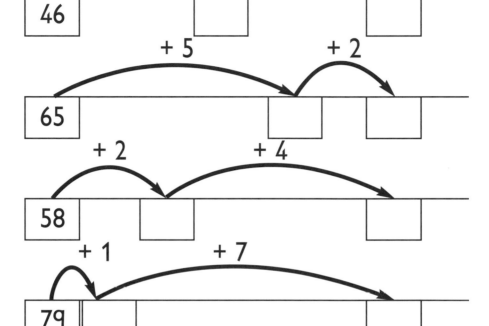

+ 5   + 2

65 ☐ ☐

| 58 + 6 |

+ 2   + 4

58 ☐ ☐

| 79 + 8 |

+ 1   + 7

79 ☐ ☐

| 47 + 8 |

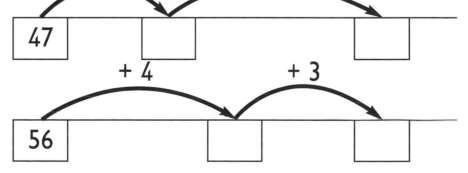

+ 3   + 5

47 ☐ ☐

| 56 + 7 |

+ 4   + 3

56 ☐ ☐

- Talk to a partner about the patterns you notice in the calculations above.

Teachers' note Encourage the children to observe how the number being added is split (partitioned) into parts to make the next multiple of 10 and that the remaining part forms the unit digit of the answer. The numbers can be masked and altered before copying to provide more variety. The following sheet can also be used to provide practice of subtractions of this type.

100% New Developing Mathematics Using and Applying Mathematics: Ages 7–8 © A & C BLACK

59

Noah's arcs (subtraction)

- **Fill in the missing numbers on each diagram to show how Noah answered each question.**

65 – 8

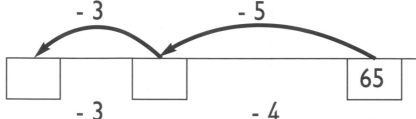
−3   −5   [ ]   [ ]   65

34 – 7

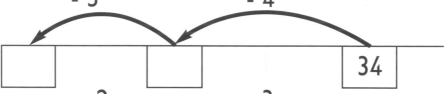
−3   −4   [ ]   [ ]   34

53 – 5

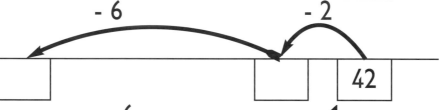
−2   −3   [ ]   [ ]   53

42 – 8

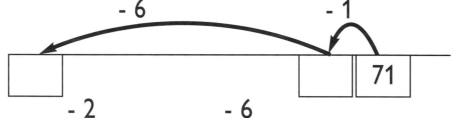
−6   −2   [ ]   [ ]   42

71 – 7

−6   −1   [ ]   [ ]   71

66 – 8

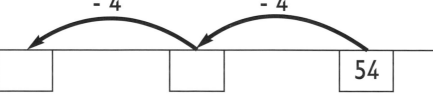
−2   −6   [ ]   [ ]   66

54 – 8

−4   −4   [ ]   [ ]   54

NOW TRY THIS!

- **Talk to a partner about the patterns you notice in the calculations above.**

Teachers' note Encourage the children to observe how the number being subtracted is split (partitioned) into parts to make the previous multiple of 10. The numbers can be masked and altered before copying to provide more variety.

100% New Developing Mathematics Using and Applying Mathematics: Ages 7–8 © A & C BLACK

Share and share alike

Some children put their money together and share it ⬚ equally ⬚.

- Predict how much they will each get.
- Work out the answer.

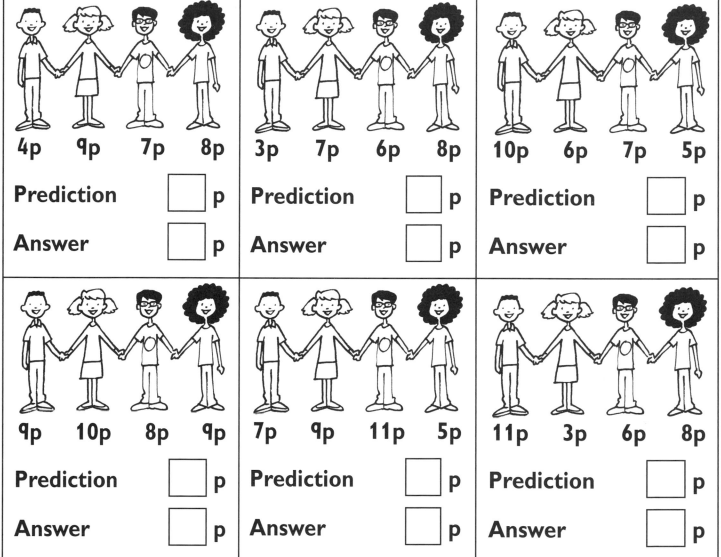

4p	9p	7p	8p

Prediction ⬚ p

Answer ⬚ p

3p	7p	6p	8p

Prediction ⬚ p

Answer ⬚ p

10p	6p	7p	5p

Prediction ⬚ p

Answer ⬚ p

9p	10p	8p	9p

Prediction ⬚ p

Answer ⬚ p

7p	9p	11p	5p

Prediction ⬚ p

Answer ⬚ p

11p	3p	6p	8p

Prediction ⬚ p

Answer ⬚ p

NOW TRY THIS!

- Talk to a partner about how you answered these.
- Can you think of a different way to do it?
- How could you record what you did so that someone else could read and understand it?

Teachers' note Discuss different strategies that could be used and the means of recording the method so that others could understand and follow it. For example, only taking money from those children with more money and giving it to those with less, or beginning with the lowest amount and making sure each child has that much, only sharing out the extra coins above this amount.

100% New Developing Mathematics Using and Applying Mathematics: Ages 7–8 © A & C BLACK

Broken keys

• **Write how you would answer each question on the calculator without using the keys marked with a** boxed{cross} **.**

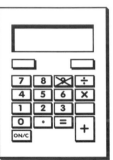

21 x 20

_____

_____

_____

99 x 12

_____

_____

_____

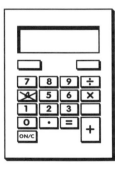

444 + 333

_____

_____

_____

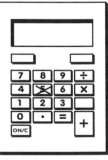

500 − 235

_____

_____

_____

104 ÷ 8

_____

_____

_____

Teachers' note These calculations require considerable thought as the children must find a way of answering the calculation without using the key marked with a cross. Encourage them to discuss their different approaches together and say which they think are most easily understood. The calculations can be altered before copying to provide differentiation and variety.

100% New Developing Mathematic
Using and Applying
Mathematics: Ages 7–8
© A & C BLACK

Answers

p 13
1 13   **2** 7   **3** 108   **4** 27   **5** 4   **6** 21

p 14
1 8   **2** 9   **3** 6   **4** 10   **5** 6   **6** 8   **7** 40   **8** 4

p 15
2, 5   3, 2
10, 4   5, 5
10, 2   10, 1
7, 5   10, 9

p 17
1 9   **2** 27   **3** 19   **4** 45   **5** 39   **6** 21   **7** 11   **8** 13

p 19
1 26 + 7 = 33
2 8 + 13 = 21
3 3 × 7 = 21
4 £3.70 × 2 + £5.80 = £13.20 or £3.70 + £3.70 + £5.80 = £13.20
5 £2.10 × 5 = £10.50
6 £23.20 ÷ £5.80 = 4 or £5.80 × [4] = £23.20
7 £23.70 ÷ £7.90 = 3 or £7.90 × [3] = £23.70
8 34 – 26 + 17 = 25
9 27 + 12 – 15 = 24
10 45 + 8 = 53

p 20
1a) £9.98   **b)** £32.97   **c)** £27.98   **d)** £15.48   **e)** £45.46   **f)** £34.96
2a) £2.03   **b)** £9.51   **c)** £2.02   **d)** £0.04 or 4p

NTT
Yes (£19.47)

p 21
The phrase from start to finish is TRY TO DANCE

p 22
1 470 mm   3 cm   **2** 790 mm   21 cm
3 63 cm   37 cm   **4** 23 cm   27 cm

NTT
51.5 cm   83.5 cm   567.5 cm 177.5 cm

p 23
1 1 kg = 500 g + 250 g + [250 g]
2 900 g ÷ 3 = [300 g]
3 2 kg = 350 g + 350 g + [1300 g]
4 900 g ÷ 2 = [450 g], 450 g – 100 g = [350 g]
5 125 g × 4 = [500 g]
6 200 g + (200 g x 3) = [800 g]

p 24
1 800 g ÷ 2 = [400 g], 400 g ÷ 2 = [200 g], 800 g + 400 g + 200 g = [1400 g]
2 2000 g – 200 g = [1800 g], 1800 ÷ 2 = [900 g]
3 2000 g – 800 = [1200 g], 1200 ÷ 2 = [600 g]
4 320 g x 2 = [640 g], 320 g + 180 g = [500 g], 640 g + 500 g = [1140 g]
5 1? kg ÷ 3 = [? kg], ? kg + 1? kg =[2 kg]
6 150 g × 4 =[600 g]

p 25
1 1:25 p.m.   **2** 2 hours 45 minutes   **3** 3:15 p.m.
4 25 minutes   **5** 40 minutes   **6** 10:35 p.m.

p 26
This is one possible solution
(all rotations of this solution
are also possible)

p 27
[16] + 12 = 28   40 – [23] = 17
[6] × 3 = 18   50 – 24 = [26]
[50] ÷ 5 = 10   [90] – 30 = 60
17 + 24 = [41]   24 ÷ 4 = [6]

p 28
16p 16
£1.05 25p
45p 24
15 24p
36p 6

p 29
90 + 15 = [ ], 15 + [ ] = 90, 90 ÷ 15 = [ ], (15 ÷ 25) + 8 = [ ]
90 – [ ] = 15, [ ] × 15 = 90, 90 ÷ 15 = [ ], 15 + [ ] = 90

p 30
100 – 25 – [ ] = 8, 1 + 8 + [ ] = 25 , 100 – 25 – [ ] = 8
100 × 8 + [ ], 100 ÷ 25 × [ ] = 8, 100 × 8 ÷ 25 = [ ]
(1 + 8) × 25 = [ ], (100 × 8) + 25 = [ ]

p 31
40 sweets

NTT
16

p 32
20 children (A = 3, B = 6, C = 1, D = 7, E = 3)

p 33
17 sheep, 10 lambs, 7 ewes

p 34
1 40 – [ ] = 15, **2** 42 ÷ 14 = [ ], **3** 24 × 3 = [ ], **4** [ ] – 14 = 11

NTT
90 ÷ 3 × 5, 35 ÷ 5 × 12

p35
The words spell:
CAP, BIN, GET, ROD

p 36
There are only 3 possible ways of making the total 8.
11114, 11123 and 11222

NTT
There are 5 possible ways of making the total 9.
1115, 11124, 11133, 11223, 12222
If the investigation is continued further here are the results:
There is 1 possible way of making the total 5.
There is 1 possible way of making the total 6.
There are 2 possible ways of making the total 7.
There are 3 possible ways of making the total 8.
There are 5 possible ways of making the total 9.
here are 7 possible ways of making the total 10.
There are 9 possible ways of making the total 11.
There are 12 possible ways of making the total 12.
There are 18 possible ways of making the total 13.

p 38
0 + 0 + 0 = 0, 0 + 0 + 1 = 1, 0 + 0 + 2 = 2, 0 + 1 + 1 = 2
0 + 1 + 2 = 3, 1 + 1 + 1 = 3, 0 + 2 + 2 = 4, 1 + 1 + 2 = 4
1 + 2 + 2 = 5, 2 + 2 + 2 = 6

For the extension activity encourage them to show the possibilities in a table like this:

+	1	2	3	4	5	6
1	2	3	4	5	6	7
2	3	4	5	6	7	8
3	4	5	6	7	8	9
4	5	6	7	8	9	10
5	6	7	8	9	10	11
6	7	8	9	10	11	12

p 42

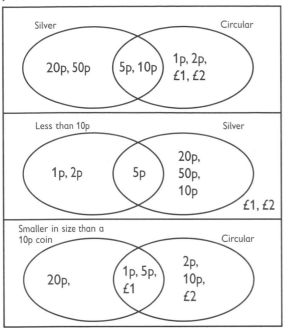

p 43
25, 3, 45, 30, 2, 20, 60, 35, 17, 8

p 44

Bong, Bing, Bang	Bing, Bong, Bang
Bong, Bang, Bing	Bang, Bong, Bing
Bing, Bang, Bong	Bang, Bing, Bong

1

Bing, Bang, Bung, Bong	Bing, Bung, Bang, Bong
Bing, Bang, Bong, Bung	Bing, Bong, Bang, Bung
Bing, Bung, Bong, Bang	Bing, Bong, Bung, Bang

2

Bong, Bang, Bung, Bing	Bong, Bung, Bang, Bing
Bong, Bang, Bing, Bung	Bong, Bing, Bang, Bung
Bong, Bung, Bing, Bang	Bong, Bing, Bung, Bang

3

Bang, Bong, Bung, Bing	Bang, Bung, Bong, Bing
Bang, Bong, Bing, Bung	Bang, Bing, Bong, Bung
Bang, Bung, Bing, Bong	Bang, Bing, Bung, Bong

4

Bung, Bong, Bang, Bing	Bung, Bang, Bong, Bing
Bung, Bong, Bing, Bang	Bung, Bing, Bong, Bang
Bung, Bang, Bing, Bong	Bung, Bing, Bang, Bong

p 46

3 × 4 − 6 = 6	5 × 3 − 6 = 9	6 × 3 − 5 = 13
4 × 3 − 6 = 6	3 × 5 − 6 = 9	3 × 6 − 5 = 13
3 × 4 − 5 = 7	5 × 3 − 4 = 11	6 × 3 − 4 = 14
4 × 3 − 5 = 7	3 × 5 − 4 = 11	3 × 6 − 4 = 14
5 × 4 − 6 = 14	6 × 4 − 5 = 19	5 × 6 − 4 = 26
4 × 5 − 6 = 14	4 × 6 − 5 = 19	6 × 5 − 4 = 26
5 × 4 − 3 = 17	6 × 4 − 3 = 21	5 × 6 − 3 = 27
4 × 5 − 3 = 17	4 × 6 − 3 = 21	6 × 5 − 3 = 27

NTT 36 more, i.e. 60 in total

p 47

1p - 1 coin,	2p - 1 coin,	3p - 2 coins ,	4p - 2 coins,
5p - 1 coin,	6p - 2 coins,	7p - 2 coins,	8p - 3 coins,
9p - 3 coins,	10p - 1 coin,	11p - 2 coins,	12p - 2 coins,
13p - 3 coins,	14p - 3 coins,	15p - 2 coins,	16p - 3 coins,
17p - 3 coins,	18p - 4 coins,	19p - 4 coins,	20p - 1 coin

NTT
28p, 29p, 33p, 34p, 36p, 37p, 38p, 39p

p 48

27 + 28 = 55	15 + 39 = 54
17 + 38 = 55	15 + 49 = 64
7 + 48 = 55	15 + 59 = 74

07 + 35 = 42

37 + 35 = 72	27 + 52 = 79
47 + 35 = 82	26 + 52 = 78

85 + 08 = 93	07 + 07 = 14
55 + 38 = 93	37 + 37 = 74
45 + 48 = 93	47 + 47 = 94

p 51
1 triangle 1 right angle
2 triangle 1 right angle
3 pentagon 2 right angles
4 square 4 right angles
5 pentagon 3 right angles
6 pentagon 3 right angles
7 pentagon 3 right angles
8 square 4 right angles

p 52
1 5 sides 3 right angles
2 7 sides 4 right angles
3 11 sides 6 right angles
4 12 sides 8 right angles
5 12 sides 7 right angles
6 12 sides 6 right angles
7 12 sides 5 right angles
8 12 sides 4 right angles

p 53
1 6   2 7   3 9   4 6   5 5   6 11   7 10   8 11

p 54
1 false   2 false   3 false   4 true   5 true   6 true

p 57
2-year-olds:

plus rotations and reflections

3-year-olds:

plus rotations and reflections

4-year-olds:

plus rotations and reflections

p 61

7p	6p	7p
9p	8p	7p

p 62
Possible calculations:

11 + 10 = [21] × 60 ÷ 3

100 × 12 − 12

333 × 2 + 111

400 − 134 − 1

104 ÷ 2 ÷ 2÷ 2

64